ADVENTURES

OF

ALF. WILSON

A THRILLING EPISODE

OF THE

DARK DAYS OF THE REBELLION

BY

JOHN A.WILSON,

A Member of the Mitchell Railroad Raiders.

WASHINGTON, D. C.
THE NATIONAL TRIBUNE.
1897.

PERSONAL.

AFTER the following chapters of this book were in type, and I thought my work completed, I received notice from the printers that two pages of space had been left for an author's preface, and a request that I should forward the same without delay.

As book-making is regulated by established customs, I suppose; that in order to please the printers and conform to these old established usages, I ought to fill these two pages with an apology for writing a book, or, rather, for my unfitness for such work. I have, in this connection, only this consoling thought to offer the reader—that had I been a better book-maker, I might have been less a Mitchell raider.

Originally, the following chapters of this book were intended solely for publication in the local newspaper of my own county. My friends and old army comrades, after reading them, as they appeared from week to week, said they were interesting and advised me to publish them in book form, and here it is. If it does not meet the requirements of the critics, let them bear in mind that it is simply the story of a private soldier, told in plain words, by one who aspires to no literary honors, who claims no credit for martyrdom, whose deeds did not change the tide of a single battle, nor to any act of soldierly gallantry. None of these are mine. I may say, too, incidentally, that stealing and wrecking a railroad, even in case of

those who succeed, is not considered an unusual occurrence, not even in times of peace, and does not usually furnish material for a book; but in this case there are a few circumstances, incidents and accidents not connected with common occurrences
of the kind. I am not, however, aware, to this day, what effect our efforts had, if any, on the stock of the Georgia Central Railroad; yet, had we succeeded, I do not think it would have been beneficial to the owners at that time. I need not, perhaps, say to the reader, that I never have had any further desire to engage in railroad enterprises, and all the credit I claim for myself, in this expedition, is that I believe I cheated the rebels out of the pleasure of hanging me, and did all in my power to carry out the orders of my General, and tried to serve my country faithfully.

I can not conscientiously close without first acknowledging valuable assistance from C. W. Evers, of the *Wood County Sentinel*, Bowling Green, Ohio, and to F. J. Oblinger, of the *Toledo Bee;* also to my comrade raiders, Robert Parrot, of Kenton, Ohio, William J. Knight, of North Pacific Junction, Minnesota, and also to comrade William Pittenger's Book, "*Daring and Suffering,*" for several points that had escaped my memory.

JOHN A. WILSON.

HASKINS, OHIO, April 26, 1880.

CONTENTS.

CHAPTER I.

CHAPTER II.

CHAPTER III.

CHAPTER IV.

CHAPTER X.

CHAPTER XI.

CHAPTER XII.

CHAPTER XIII.

CHAPTER XIV.

INTRODUCTION.

IN the quiet little village of Haskins, Wood County, Ohio, lives the subject of these adventures—a modest, quiet, unpretentious gentleman, a good citizen, in whose outward appearance and actions there is nothing to indicate to the casual observer that he was one of a band of men of more than Spartan valor, who, in the midst of one of the darkest periods of the nation's annals, participated in one of the most thrilling incidents of a gigantic war—a war whose history is one of Titanic death-struggles, where thousands of brave men with the most improved contrivances and implements of warfare of modern times, strove for the mastery—a war marked from beginning to end with startling dramatic acts of adventure and heroism, unsurpassed in the annals of the world. The ancient chroniclers of Greece and Rome tell us of prodigious feats of valor in arms, while the historian of modern times excites our admiration with the military genius of Napoleon and the bravery and devotion of his marshals and soldiers. The legends of Scotland teem with the stories of patriotism, devotion, and self-sacrifice of that brave people; but it is no disparagement to say of all these that in acts of patriotism, devotion, daring, endurance, and all the qualities which go to make the soldier, history gives no account of men superior to those developed by the war of the American Rebellion. Lord Nelson, the hero of Trafalgar, and the idol of the British nation, was not braver than Farragut, lashed to the mast of his ship in Mobile Bay, and Cambronne and the Imperial Guard at Waterloo were not braver than Pickett, who led the dreadful charge at Gettysburg, and the men who followed him.

When the actors in the bloody drama of the Rebellion shall all have, passed away, and personal jealousies and sectional animosities have died out, then will history make an impartial award of merits to the actors in that great struggle. Much that was real and dreadful will then read like fiction and romance, as if it had occurred in the days of miracles and wonders. The timely arrival of the little Monitor at Hampton Roads, and her combat and miraculous victory over the monster iron-clad Merrimac, or the providential rain-fall which delayed one day Albert Sidney Johnston's attack on Grant at Shiloh, thereby saving, the Union army, are events so familiar to this, generation that they seem commonplace; yet they are events, small as they may seem, on which, perhaps, hung the fate of the Republic. The whole war, from its beginning to its close, ending in the tragic death of the Chief Executive of the nation, was a succession of startling events, deeds of valor, great battles, hard marches, victories, defeats, and adventure by land and sea, which put to the sorest test the powers of endurance and bravery of the combatants.

The mettle of the hero of the following pages, although not tasted on the battle-field amid the rattle of musketry, the boom of cannon, the shriek of shot and shell, and the soul-inspiring strains of martial music, was tried in a crucible where coolness, courage, fortitude, endurance, valor, nerve that amounted almost to sublimity, were called into requisition, and where all the ennobling traits of man's highest nature were brought into play. This trying ordeal will be fully developed, in the pages that follow.

John A. Wilson was born July 25, 1832, near the town of

Worthington, Franklin County, Ohio. When a boy about seventeen years of age, he removed with his father, Ezekiel Wilson, to Wood County, the family locating not far from Haskins, where the lad Wilson grew to manhood.

With the exception of a year's residence in Iowa, and his term of army service, Mr. Wilson, or "Alf.," as all his acquaintances call him, has since been a resident of Wood County. In stature he is medium, weighing, perhaps, one hundred and fifty pounds, of rather slender, but wiry, build, of nervous temperament, light hair, and bluish grey eyes. In his manner he is deliberate, though quick of decision and action, and there is that in his appearance that denotes to the close observer of human character a fearless determination and tenacity of purpose that can not be swerved without sufficient reason. He is a man somewhat after the old John Brown make-up in tenacity of resolution, belief and purpose. Though broken in health, having endured and suffered enough to break the strongest constitution, he is yet active in mind and body, being one of those persons who will never cease to be active until overtaken by the last enemy of mankind. On the subject of his many startling adventures, his perilous hardships, and hairbreadth escapes, he is usually reticent. When he is induced to speak of them, the dark hours of his imprisonment seem to harrow up his feelings to their utmost tension. His eyes dance with an unnatural light, he grows excitedly nervous over the recollections of that terrible summer, and his every action indicates that of a tempest-tossed spirit over the bitter memories of the past. Under no other circumstances is this state of mental incandescence perceivable with Mr. Wilson. It is a matter of no surprise, then, that a man of his temperament should so seldom allude to the bitter agonies and harrowing circumstances of that memorable year.

At the beginning of the Rebellion, in 1861, Mr. Wilson

enlisted in C Company, Twenty-First Ohio Volunteer Infantry, and the ever-shifting events of the war found the regiment, of which Colonel J. S. Norton, now of Toledo, was commander, stationed near Shelbyville, Tennessee, and in the army division commanded by that enterprising and far-seeing officer, General O. M. Mitchell, who was then directing his column to Chattanooga. This was in April, 1862, and it is at this point that the adventures of Mr. Wilson properly begin. In order, however, to get a better understanding of the importance of the perilous enterprise about to be related, and its direct bearing on the gigantic military operations then transpiring, it will be well to briefly recapitulate a little of the history of that period.

General McClellan, at that time, was advancing on Richmond in the east. In the west, General Grant had just gained a great victory at Fort Donelson. This defeat of the Confederates caused them to virtually abandon Kentucky and Western and Middle Tennessee. The Federal forces promptly followed up their advantage and advanced their army up the Tennessee River, by gunboats and transports, as far as Pittsburg Landing. To meet this powerful array of the Federal armies, the Confederate Generals, Johnson and Beauregard, were making superhuman efforts to concentrate a Confederate force at Corinth, powerful enough to meet and crush Grant's army before it advanced further southward. Troops and supplies were being hurried forward from all directions; but from no place was the supply so strong and steady as from the State of Georgia, the granary of the South. This stream of constant supply and fresh levies came from Georgia by the Memphis & Charleston Railroad. Corinth, where the Rebel army lay, is situated on this Railroad, and so is Chattanooga, though the two places are a long distance apart. From Chattanooga south to Atlanta, the heart of Georgia, the traffic was over the Georgia State Railroad. Over this Railroad, Georgia and other portions of the Gulf territory not only sent supplies to the Confederate forces preparing for battle at Corinth, but over the East Tennessee and Virginia Railroad, by way of Chattanooga, to Richmond and to Cumberland Gap, then threatened by General George W. Morgan, with a Federal division. From this it will be seen that the Georgia State Road, from Atlanta and the South, intersecting, as it did at Chattanooga, roads running to Virginia and to the west, distributing supplies and troops on shortest notice at points where most needed, was a most important and essential factor to the success of the Confederates, in resisting the great armies which menaced them in Virginia and the Gulf States.

The Federal Generals foresaw the importance of destroying, even temporarily, this great artery of supply to the Confederates. But to attempt it with a large force would be extremely hazardous, as it would necessarily place such force hundreds of miles from its base of supplies, and with its line of communication in the control of the Confederates.

Some time in March, a noted Union spy, or secret service agent, named J. J. Andrews, a Kentuckian by birth, and who had repeatedly visited all portions of the South and was thoroughly familiar with the railroad in question, discussed with General Mitchell the possibility of accomplishing the work with a *secret* expedition. General Mitchell soon became interested in the bold proposition, and, after due consideration, fell in with the plan. Eight men voluntarily started out on the perilous enterprise, but after an absence of some days, they all returned without attempting the hazardous undertaking. But Andrews was loth to give up his daring project, and subsequently had a consultation with General Mitchell, in whicn he claimed that the project was still feasible. General Mitchell with some misgivings, continued to favor it, because the scheme, if successful would cripple the Confederates and send terror and dismay through the whole Confederacy; and it was one of those problematical, far-reaching undertakings, in which this restless officer seemed to delight. But he did not like the possible consequences which might fall on the heads of the men who would have to go with Andrews on the dangerous expedition, in case of failure. He knew if they were captured they would be executed. However, the General gave Andrews permission to make the attempt, provided he could find twenty men among the regiments of the division who would voluntarily go with him. This, strange as it may seem, was not attended with any great trouble, hazardous as was to be the service. The army abounded in cool-headed, daring spirits, and in a short time the list of volunteers was made up, to the number of twenty-four, including Andrews, the leader.

Such was the origin of one of the most daring exploits conceived during the War of the Rebellion—one which for boldness of design, intrepidity, daring and recklessness, has but few parallels in the history of ancient or modern warfare.

Hon. Judge Holt, in his official report as Secretary of War, used these words: "The expedition, in the daring of its conception, had the wildness of a romance; while in the gigantic and overwhelming results it sought and was likely to accomplish, it was absolutely sublime."

And with this introduction to the details of this thrilling expedition, necessary to a proper understanding of the events about to be related, Mr. Wilson will take up the narrative, which has all the sensation of a thrilling romance, and yet in which there is not a line that is not true to the letter.

C. W. E.

ADVENTURES OF ALF. WILSON.

CHAPTER I.

First Meeting of the Raiders near Shelbyville—Their Names—Putting on Citizens' Clothes—Andrews, the Federal Spy—Final Instructions and Farewell by General Mitchell—We Break into Squads and are Off to Dixie—Wayside Reflections—Heavy Rains and Freshets in the Rivers—"Meeting Up" with a True Union Man—Our Story of Deception—An Old Rebel Colonel—A Confederate Spy—Crossing the Cumberland Mountains—Safe Arrival at Chattanooga—One Day Behind Time—Off to Marietta by Rail.

"With years, ye know, have not declined
My strength, my courage, or my mind,
Or at this hour I should not be
Telling stories beneath a tree."

IT was a pleasant day in April in the year 1862, the very day on which the bloody battle of Shiloh was fought and won (the 7th), that a party of twenty-four men assembled near the old town of Shelbyville, Tennessee, and placed themselves under the leadership of one of their number, J. J. Andrews, a daring and successful Federal spy and secret service agent.

These men, with two exceptions, were enlisted soldiers, and belonged to the division of General Ormsby M. Mitchell, then encamped about Shelbyville.

Their enrollment was as follows:

J. J. ANDREWS and WILLIAM CAMPBELL, citizens of Kentucky;

MARION A. ROSS and PERRY G. SHADRACK, Company A, Second Regiment O. V. I.;

GEORGE D. WILSON, Company B, same regiment;

WILLIAM PITTENGER, Company G, same regiment;

J. R. PORTER, MARK WOOD and J. A. WILSON, Company C, Twenty-First Regiment O. V. I.;

WILLIAM KNIGHT, Company E, same regiment;

WILSON W. BROWN, Company F, same regiment;

WILLIAM BENSINGER, Company G, same regiment;

ROBERT BUFFUM, Company H, same regiment;

JOHN SCOTT and E. H. MASON, Company K, same regiment;

M. J. HAWKINS, Company A, Thirty-Third Regiment O. V. I.;

WILLIAM REDDICK, Company B, same regiment;

JOHN WOLLAM, Company C, same regiment;

SAMUEL ROBINSON, Company G, same regiment;

D. A. DORSEY, Company H, same regiment;

JACOB PARROTT, Company K, same regiment;

SAMUEL SLAVENS, same regiment.

Two others, whose names have escaped my memory, started with us from Shelbyville, but they reached the Tennessee River so far behind the remainder of the party, as I afterwards learned, that they saw their services would be of no avail, and the next best thing was to return to the Federal lines, if possible. This they failed to do, were conscripted into the rebel army, and after some time one of them escaped back to the Federal camp, which caused suspicion to fall upon his comrade, who was arrested and afterwards placed in prison in Chattanooga.

The object of our expedition as already foreshadowed was to penetrate the rebel lines to the city of Marietta Georgia, there to secure a train of cars, by fair means or by force, and then to run northward toward our own lines, burning all the bridges and destroying the road in such a manner as to utterly and effectually break all rail communication by this most important railroad to the South. To do this successfully it was necessary to disguise ourselves in citizens' clothes. Accordingly, late in the afternoon of April 7, we went into the town of Shelbyville and procured suits of clothes, after which we assembled at a point designated for our final start. We passed through our line of pickets without difficulty, as they had been previously instructed to allow us to pass. Soon after passing our pickets we were joined by General Mitchell, and after proceeding a short distance to a secluded spot, we were halted for final instructions. This business over, the good old General took us each by the hand and with tearful eyes bade us good-bye, saying, as he did so, that he feared he should never see us again.

Before proceeding further, I will briefly describe our leader, Andrews. He was a noble specimen of manhood, nearly six feet in height, of powerful build, long raven black hair, black silken beard, Roman features, a high, expansive forehead, yet with a voice soft and gentle as that of a woman. He was a man who combined intelligence and refinement with cool, dauntless courage that quailed under no difficulty or danger. He was a man deliberate in speech and calm in manner—

a man well fitted for the dangerous service he was engaged in, though I doubt his entire fitness to command men in sudden and unexpected emergencies. However, he shared his chances equally with us, and died the death of a brave man. No braver, truer man ever lived.

Having been supplied by Andrews with Confederate money to pay our expenses, we separated into squads of four or five and directed our course toward Chattanooga, distant one hundred and three miles. We were soon clear of all our picket and vidette posts and in the enemy's country. Not until fairly away from sight of the old flag and our regiments and entirely within the enemy's line, could we begin to realize the great responsibility we had incurred. To begin with, we had cast aside our uniforms and put on citizens' clothes, and assumed all the penalties that in military usages the word SPY implies, which is death the world over. Again, our mission was such that concealment was impossible. We were sure to arouse the whole Confederacy and invoke all the brutal vengeance of its frenzied leaders in case we did not make good our escape after doing our work. The military spy, in the ordinary line of his duty, is not compelled to expose himself to detection. On the contrary, he conceals, in every possible way, his identity. This we could do until in the heart of the enemy's country, the very place where we would be in most danger and where the blow would fall most heavily on our enemies and arouse against us all their hatred and most active energies.

All these things passed in review in our minds as we walked on, but did not cause us to slacken our pace or

GOOD-BY TO GEN. MITCHEL.

abate our will and determination to destroy the Georgia State Railroad or die in the attempt. There was, I may say right here, one thought about the business that I did not just like—that if caught I would die the death of a spy—be hung. I had enlisted as a soldier and of course knew that I took in the bargain some chances of being shot, which is not a dishonorable way of closing up a soldier's earthly account. I speak of this, that the reader may in some measure appreciate the perplexing anxiety of our situation at times, and also as an explanation of some things which subsequently occurred, and which may appear to have been done in wanton bravado, or with a reckless disregard of life.

It commenced raining again the night of our departure, as it had done the week previous, and continued with but very little cessation during our entire trip. This of itself increased the obstacles that delayed us.

During our first day's march we met, for a wonder, a true Southern Union man—as loyal a man as ever I met. He was an old man, who had remained true, though surrounded by disloyal neighbors. Though we professed to be rebels on our way to enlist in the rebel army, he boldly spoke his sentiments and did his best to persuade us to return and cast our lot with the Union army. After much urging he piloted us to the river, which was so swollen by rain that we could not ford it as we expected. The whole face of the country was a vast sheet of water, and we waded for miles through mud and water. The old man procured us a skiff, and we then, with a hearty shake of his loyal hand, bade him farewell.

Our instructions we were allowed just four days,

not only to reach Chattanooga, but to accomplish the work. The continued rains and bad roads made this accomplishment in the allotted time simply an impossibility. It delayed us one day longer than the time agreed upon, and had much to do with the outcome of our undertaking, as will be hereafter seen. That old adage which says, "Delays are dangerous," was most faithfully verified in our case.

During our journey to Chattanooga, Andrews, who was mounted, would ride ahead and make all necessary inquiries and then, passing out of sight, would allow us to go by, when he would mount and overtake us in some safe place where he would give us instructions, and then ride on, as though we were entire strangers to him and he to us. He would frequently pass us, simply bidding us the time in a careless way, and perhaps in an indifferent manner would ask us which way we were traveling. Sometimes, when squads of rebels were about, he would ask us where we were going. The reply would invariably be—

"To Chattanooga, sir."

"Are you soldiers?"

"No, sir, we are not soldiers, but we expect to be as soon as we can get to one of the Kentucky regiments. We are from Kentucky and are on the way to join the army, sir. We have become so disgusted with the cussed Yankees since they came into our State, that we can't stand it any longer, and we are determined to fight them as long as there is a man left. They have ruined our State, sir. Yes, sir, they steal everything they can lay their hands on; they have burned nearly every fence in the State, sir. Are you acquainted in

Chattanooga, sir? Could you give us any information about Colonel Williams' regiment?"

"No, men, I'm sorry to say I can't, now; but I'm glad to see you come out to fight for your country. The Lincolnites are determined to take all our slaves from us, confiscate our homes, and cut our throats in the bargain. It is the duty of every Southern man to rally to arms and drive them from our country."

During these conversations the rebel citizens would look on and by their actions and words they seemed to think we were as good Confederates as ever lived. In this manner we were able to travel through their country without exciting suspicion.

On Wednesday night, April 9, we arrived at the little village of Manchester. Near this village some of the party stopped for the night at the house of an old rebel who bore the title of Colonel. It was our plan to avoid persons of his stamp, as we did not care to undergo too close scrutiny. But night overtook a part of the squad there and none who took shelter under the old Colonel's roof had cause to feel sorry. He was a good entertainer, had plenty of the comforts of life about him and was an incessant talker, especially on the subject uppermost in his mind—the war. He was at first a little cautious and shy, but on being assured that his guests were Confederates of the best stripe, he relaxed himself and assured them that he felt honored by their presence and that it was a privilege indeed to be able to serve such brave men—men who were patriotic enough to leave their homes in Old Kentucky and go voluntarily to the front in the great hour of danger. It did not seem as though he could do enough for the boys; nothing he had was too good. He proved his loyalty, the next morning, to the secession cause, and his good will to them by taking his team and wagon and hauling them as far as the mountains, to a little place called Pelham. While in his company we had no reason to fear suspicion. No better guarantee that we were all right was needed in that part of Tennessee. Before leaving the men he took them to a tavern and treated them to whisky, after which he bade them good speed and returned home. Whether he ever learned his mistake or not I do not know.

For myself, I spent the same night with an old farmer—a neighbor of the old Colonel's—a mild and inoffensive-appearing old man. I was very hungry and tired and felt great gratification on seating myself at his table to see it so bountifully supplied with substantial eatables so tempting to a hungry man. I ate heartily and said but few words. There was a rather genteel, smooth-looking man at the table whose presence and appearance I did not exactly understand. I could not at first make out whether he belonged to the place or not, but soon discovered that he was a stranger. I kept a discreet tongue and learned bye and bye that the stranger, too, was on his way to Chattanooga. He inquired particularly concerning the roads and very minutely in regard to the Yankees. The old man told him that *he* had never seen a Yankee nor heard of any being nearer than the coal banks at the mountains. The stranger seemed quite uneasy lest he should fall into Yankee hands and was evidently no lover of the horrible "Yanks." Next morning, in good season, we were ready to continue our journey and the stranger became one of our traveling companions. He did not long continue with us, however, as we took a road that was supposed to come in close proximity to the Federal lines. He now took me one side and proposed to give me forty dollars to pilot him over the mountains. He told me he was a spy, acting in the employ of the Confederate Government.

My mind was now thrown into a cloud of doubt and perplexity as to what was the proper thing to do. At times I had a mind to accept his offer and go as a guide with him until I had a chance to lose him or get separated from him. He might, in case he had seen reason to suspect us, get to Chattanooga in advance of us and cause our arrest and imprisonment. I was at no little loss what to do. At one time I had concluded to go with him until we could reach some secluded place and there treat him to the fate of a spy and enemy of my country—a fate he deserved, as I knew he was carrying important news to the Confederates. But on the other hand, if I did this, it might detain me so long that I would fail to be on time to discharge my part in the service for which I had been detailed. We finally let him go his road and we went ours. When we arrived in Chattanooga he was the first man we met and he, supposing us to be friends, treated us with great cordiality and invited us to go with him and "have something," but it was nearly train time and we had reasons for politely declining, not caring to make his further acquaintance. This was the last we saw of the nice-appearing stranger and Confederate spy.

We reached the north bank of the Tennessee River, opposite Chattanooga, on Friday, the 11th, one day behind the time agreed upon with General Mitchell, and were compelled to wait for some time for the wind to subside so that the ferry-boat—a little, crazy, frail affair—could carry us safely across. At length, however, we had the satisfaction of landing safe and sound in Chattanooga, where we found we had been preceded by most of the party. We went to the depot and purchased tickets to Marietta, Georgia. Some of the party purchased several tickets, so that there would not be so many of us at the office at once. Everything thus far appeared to work finely. We all secured our tickets, went aboard the train, and no one seemed to pay any attention to us. This was a great relief to us. We took seats in the cars and were soon moving off into Dixie at a good rate of speed. I felt that this was a much easier and more expeditious way of getting on than the tedious, tiresome march of the previous four days.

After getting seated, and there being no further cause of concern for the time being, I began to carefully study over the situation with all the thought I could, and to calculate our chances of success or failure, and the result of my deliberations was by no means encouraging. We were one day behind the time appointed. I knew, too, or felt sure, that General Mitchell would not fail to march upon and take Huntsville, according to the arrangements made with us when we started. I also felt certain that if he did so there would be little room to hope for our success. It would cause the road to be crowded with trains flying from danger, and it would be difficult for us to pass them all in safety. But it was too late now to change the programme. We must make the effort, come what might. I said nothing, however, to any one except Andrews; but on listening to my opinion on the situation he encouraged me by saying there was yet a good chance to succeed. Indeed, he expressed himself in so sanguine a manner that I made no further argument; but I still thought my course of reasoning correct, whether the result would accord with it or not.

CHAPTER II.

Safe Arrival at Marietta—On Board the Morning Express—Porter and Hawkins get Left—Capturing the Train at Big Shanty—A Bewildered Multitude of Rebels—We Pull Out Lively—Cutting Telegraph Wires—Tearing up Railroad Track—The Powder Train Story—Almost a Row with the Train Men—A Zealous Station Agent, who was Willing to Send his Last Shirt to General Beauregard—Hindered by Down Trains Fleeing from General Mitchell—Pursued by a Locomotive—Tearing up More Track—A Railroad Race for Life or Death—Vain Efforts to Impede Pursuit—Trying to Burn a Bridge—Throwing off Ties on the Track—A Reckless and Devil-may-care Race, the Like of Which was Never Before Seen.

"Now, by St. Paul, the work goes bravely on."

WE left Chattanooga a little while before sunset, and arrived at Marietta soon after midnight, a distance of one hundred and thirty miles. We at once repaired to the nearest hotel and registered, of course giving fictitious names. Before retiring, arrangements were made to have the hotel men awake us in time for the north-bound train in the morning, which they promised to do without fail.

No man knows what a day may bring forth; and this very uncertainty of what the light of that day's sun would bring forth in our particular cases was the reason some of us, myself at least of the number, did not sleep very much. Our doom might be fixed before the setting of another sun. We might be hanging to the limbs of some of the trees along the railroad, with an enraged populace jeering and shouting epithets and vengeance because we had no more lives to give up; or, we might leave a trail of fire and destruction behind us and come triumphantly rolling into Chattanooga and Huntsville, within the Federal lines, to receive the welcome plaudits of comrades left behind, and the thanks of our General and the praises of a grateful people. Such thoughts as these passed in swift review, and were not well calculated to make one sleep soundly. But even this broken rest was not to continue long. The two or three hours soon slipped by and we were called and notified to "hurry up or we would be left." Two of our men who lodged at another house, Porter and Hawkins, by some mistake, were not called, and were left, so that only twenty of us took the train. This was a serious loss, for Hawkins was the most experienced engineer of the party, and he was the one selected to take charge of the engine; but it is not likely that the result of the expedition would have been different, even with his practice and experience.

The reader will, by glancing at a map of Georgia, notice that just to the north of Marietta, on the railroad, are the towns of Kenesaw and Big Shanty. Sherman's soldiers will all remember these two places. It was the latter place, also called Camp McDonald, a place where rebel recruits in great numbers were brought for organization and drill, that had been selected to strike the first blow, by capturing the train, or such portion of it as was wanted. Big Shanty is only eight or ten miles from Marietta, and there were two good reasons why we selected that particular station. In the first place, there was no telegraph office there—an important point in our favor—and in the next place it was a lunch station, where passengers were allowed twenty minutes for refreshments. This was in our favor, for it might save us the necessity of killing the engineer and fireman, who would, in all probability, leave the engine to go to the refreshment room. Aside from considerations of humanity, it was our wish to avoid any collision or delay, for there were camped within sight of the station no less than ten thousand Confederates.

The train we had taken passage on was the express, heavily loaded with passengers and drawn by a fine looking locomotive. There was many an anxious gaze from one to another of our party after we had taken our seats in the cars that morning, as if to read the thoughts of each, as men will sometimes do when drawn up in line on the eve of a great battle when the skirmishers are slowly retreating before the advancing columns of the enemy. For my own part I could not discover on a face in our party any sign of trepidation or timidity. Each seemed cool, decided and resolute. Few words were spoken and each seemed impatient for the decisive moment to arrive. When the shrill whistle announced that we had arrived at the station and the conductor sang out "Big Shanty! twenty minutes for breakfast!" and himself started for the restaurant, followed by the engineer and fireman, we felt a happy relief. The passengers were swarming into the eating-house for breakfast pell-mell. Now was our time to strike!

Our party had, by this time, all drifted together along side the train on the platform, when Andrews, who had been ahead to see if the switches were all right and the track clear, came up and quietly said, "All right, boys." Every man sprang to his place. Andrews, who had been improving all his time, had uncoupled the train, leaving three box-cars hitched to the tender. Andrews, Brown, Knight and myself sprang on the engine. Knight grasped the lever of the engine and gave it a surge and the ponderous wheels were instantly in motion. We were off. The rest of the men had leaped into one of the box-cars. The rebel guards who were on duty about the platform, did not at first seem to comprehend what was up, and, when it was, alas, too late, looked after us in blank amazement. We shot out lively for a short distance, perhaps nearly half a mile, as Knight had thrown the valve wide open, when we discovered the engine had been left with but little steam or fire either. We were compelled to come to a dead stop, and the way we put in wood and poured on oil wasn't slow by any means. We could see the surprised, dumbfounded crowd—citizens, soldiers, officers and railroad men—gazing after us and running hither and thither in helpless confusion. Several squads of soldiers, with their guns, started for us on the dead run, yelling like wild Comanches. Our fire was burning briskly by this time and we had no fear of them. We waited, however, until they came within thirty or forty rods and then pulled the lever and rolled out slowly for some distance, until we could gain a good head of steam. When they saw we had steam up, they came to a halt and opened a lively musketry fire on us.

They did us no harm, and every revolution of the big wheels carried us farther beyond their reach. When we were safely out of their way, we halted again and John Scott, with the agility, intrepidity and daring for which he was noted, climbed a pole and cut the telegraph wire, so that by no possibility would they be able to send a dispatch ahead of us. We then pulled out at a rapid rate for a time, until, coming to a curve in the road, we stopped again.

Every man fully realized the danger of the terrible work of destruction that we had undertaken, and was fully nerved for the struggle. Here, too, we tore up the track behind us, and Scott again cut down the wires, as he continued, to do throughout that terrible race, and this time made them fast to the rear car of the train. The way we "yanked" down telegraph poles and tore the wire loose when we started up, was frightful to behold. At the next station we met and passed a train. They evidently regarded us with surprise or suspicion. The train men knew the locomotive we were on, but the hands were all strangers to them. Besides, we were a wild train ahead of the express and unannounced. But we did not parley or answer questions nor stop until we reached the tank, where we took on water and wood. Then we pulled out at rapid speed for a while when we again stopped and tore up the track and cut the wires to cut off pursuit. We continued in this manner, destroying track and wire frequently, until we reached a little station called Marengo, where we had to stop for a southbound train to pass.

When we made the first stop, after capturing the

TEARING UP TRACKS.

train and getting clear of Big Shanty, Andrews was overjoyed at our success, and when he jumped off the locomotive he clasped each of us by the hand, congratulating us that the worst part of the job was over, as we had but one more train to pass when the "coast would all be clear." This probably would all have been true had we been one day sooner.

While we were waiting at Marengo, Andrews went into the office and procured the switch keys and a schedule, telling the office-man that he was running an "extra" through with powder and ammunition to Beauregard, who was hard pressed by Grant and was out of ammunition, and the greatest possible haste was necessary. This story, trumped up on the spur of the moment, had much semblance of truth, although we did not know it.

Not a week had elapsed since the battle of Shiloh, and Generals Grant and Halleck were at that very time pushing their columns on toward Beauregard at Corinth, and to give further plausibility to our story, there was in the express car a prodigious iron-bound safe, containing probably a wagon load of Confederate scrip, with which to pay off the Confederates at Corinth. This was satisfactory to the man, who said he would willingly take off his shirt and send it to Beauregard if it would do any good. When Andrews returned to the train we were in a great turmoil. This was the station where the express train changed hands, and no sooner had we come to a halt than the relief came on to take possession. Finding a new and strange set of men and no passenger cars, they did not know what to make of it. They knew the locomotive and asked us what we were doing on that engine? We told them the same story that Andrews told; but still they seemed to think something was not right. When Andrews, however, who was clothed in somewhat of a military dress, made his appearance and told them the same story in his serious and impressive way; that he had charge of the train and that it was very important that there should be no delay, and also assured them that the express train would be along soon, they seemed a little more reconciled. In the meantime the down train had passed, and without further parley we pulled out and left them to settle the matter the best they could.

We did not run far until we again stopped and tore up the track and cut the wires. This time we took the displaced rails with us for the purpose of making them all the trouble and delay we could, knowing that in all probability pursuit would soon follow. Thus we proceeded, tearing up the track, cutting the wires and waiting for trains to pass, frequently, however, doubling on schedule time between stations. What gave us most concern was the fact that every train that passed us carried a red flag, indicating that other trains were following. We knew the explanation of this. General Mitchell, prompt to fulfill his agreement with us, had pushed the Federal troops forward to the railroad at Huntsville, and the whole rebel population were badly scared, while all the public property was being run into Georgia for safety.

At length we reached a station where we were almost positive that we should pass the last train. Andrews went into the station where the keys were hanging and took them to adjust the switch without asking any one.

This liberty on his part was likely to raise some trouble with the station men, but the plausible powder story quieted them. After waiting a short time the down train passed, but it carried the inevitable red flag. This was not encouraging to us. Our precious time was being fatally consumed with these delays. We felt and knew it.

Finally, while we were engaged in tearing up the track, we were startled by the shrill whistle of a pursuing locomotive, away in our rear, but unmistakably coming toward us. We were followed and there was not a doubt of it. The pursuing train, however, was delayed by meeting the train which had just passed us and this delay gave us quite a start again, which we improved to the best possible advantage. It must be remembered that from the nature of our position we had a poor chance of providing ourselves with bars, saws, grappling-hooks, axes, sledges, powder, torpedoes, and other necessary implements for making quick work in the destruction of track and bridges. We had put our main reliance on destroying by fire.

Right here I may as well explain briefly, although a little out of the regular order, how the pursuit, which began at Big Shanty, was conducted. The engineer, conductor and track-master followed on a hand-car until they met the first train we had passed. They boarded this train, reversed the engine and pushed on with all possible haste. When they came to where we had displaced the track, they took up rails behind them and laid them down again in front and thus pressed on with no great delay, for on reaching the first station they dropped off most of the cars, took on a quantity of rails and a gang of track-hands and then pushed rapidly on.

When we found that we were pursued we knew that the destruction of a bridge was the only thing that would save us and to do this we must outrun them far enough to burn the bridge before they came up.

Now followed a trial of speed between locomotives —a race which for desperate, dare-devil recklessness, velocity and the high stakes at issue was never equaled on land or water on the American continent. This was our last shuffle of the cards and the game was a desperate one. It was swift vengeance on the one side and life or death on the other.

Our locomotive was under a full head of steam. The engineer stood with his hand on the lever with the valve wide open. It was frightful to see how the powerful iron monster under us would leap forward under the revolutions of her great wheels. Brown would scream to me ever and anon, "Give her more wood, Alf!" which command was promptly obeyed. She rocked and reeled like a drunken man, while we tumbled from side to side like grains of pop-corn in a hot frying-pan. It was bewildering to look at the ground, or objects on the road-side. A constant stream of fire ran from the rims of the great wheels and to this day I shudder when I reflect on that, my first and last locomotive ride. We sped past stations, houses and fields and out of sight almost like a meteor, while the bystanders who barely caught a glimpse of us as we passed, looked on as if in both fear and amazement. It has always been a wonder with me that our locomotive and cars kept the track at all, or how they could possibly stay on the track. At times the iron horse seemed literally to fly over the course, the driving-wheels of one side being lifted from the rails much of the distance over which we now sped with a velocity fearful to contemplate. We took little thought of the matter then. Death in a railroad smash-up would have been preferable to us to capture. We had but this choice left us.

While we on the locomotive were making this pell-mell, "devil-may-care" race, the men in the box-cars were not idle. They had, previous to leaving the last stopping place, taken on a lot of ties which they placed in the rear car. They then broke a large hole in the car and as we sped on would now and then drop out a tie to impede the progress of the pursuers. So great was our speed that sometimes when one of these ties struck the track it bounded twenty or thirty feet high and came whirling end over end after the train as though shot after us from a cannon.

Twice or thrice did we stop to burn bridges, but in spite of the terrible speed we had made, only a few minutes would elapse before we could hear our pursuers thundering after us like a roaring storm-cloud before a furious wind. They had in the meantime picked up another passenger locomotive and train just in from the Rome branch of the Georgia road, which, with troops, was following close after the first train.

We were now nearing Dalton, and, discovering the track all clear, we went through at a high rate of speed. Here is the only instance, I think, where we failed to do all that could have been done. We ran about two minutes too long before we stopped to cut the wire. I tried, and even insisted with Andrews, that we should stop the train sooner, but for some unknown reason he did not. It was all owing to this that our pursuers got a dispatch through to Chattanooga ahead of us. They had taken up a telegraph operator who was put off near Dalton, and who succeeded in getting a dispatch through about two minutes before we cut down the wire. I have since learned that the dispatch caused the wildest stampede in Chattanooga. Troops were called to arms, the railroad track torn up and cannon planted covering the track, while a double guard was kept on duty all night. As matters turned out, however, it made but little difference, except to scare the Chattanooga people nearly out of their senses.

We had now arrived at a part of the road which we particularly wished to destroy. We therefore determined to make another effort to burn a bridge, knowing that if we could destroy one we would be safe from our pursuers, while we could destroy the rest. Otherwise we would certainly fail. We kindled a fire in the rear car and put the locomotive again at full speed, so as to have all the time possible for the bridge to get well to burning before the pursuing train came up. We dropped off this burning car on the bridge when we reached it, and stopped to assist the fire in the work of destruction all we could. But we were not permitted to accomplish the task. We no more than fairly got to work before we saw the black smoke of the pursuing locomotive rolling above the trees as she came thundering down the road at almost lightning speed. They seemed to know our design on the bridge and were straining every nerve to foil the attempt. They had

A CLOSE PURSUIT.

one of the best locomotives on the road, and had a fresh supply of wood and water, while we had but little of either, our supply having nearly run out.

Our situation was becoming more unpleasant every moment. The road was very rough here; but, rough or smooth, our last thread of hope hung on the swiftness of our tired locomotive. We crammed the furnace with every combustible we could lay hands on. Again she plunged ahead at frightful speed, reeling and rocking on the rough track like a drunken man. We made a sudden halt at a tank and wood-pile, and hastily proceeded to "wood and water." We had, however, secured only a partial supply when the chasing train came in sight, loaded with armed soldiers.

Our pursuers were worked up to an infuriated pitch of excitement and rent the very air with their devilish screeches and yells as they came in sight of us, like dogs when the quarry is sprung. They opened on us at long range with musketry. The bullets rattled around us like hail, but fortunately none of our party was hit. This is the only instance I have ever heard of where troops were put into action on a moving railroad train and I am clear in my mind that this kind of warfare will never become popular if everybody regards it from my standpoint.

Our iron horse was now put to its severest test, but our most strenuous efforts to place distance between ourselves and our pursuers were in vain. Their locomotive was equal to ours and they were running it equally as reckless. We had nothing left on board to throw off and thus obstruct the track as we had previously done. It was becoming more evident every moment that our only and last hope lay in an abandonment of the locomotive and fleeing to the woods. Already our speed began to slacken—we had neither wood, water nor oil. The locomotive shook and reeled as she sped on. I could liken her condition to nothing else than the last struggles of a faithful horse, whose heartless master has driven and lashed him until he is gasping for breath and literally dying in the harness. The powerful machine had carried us safely for more than a hundred miles, some of the time at a rate of speed appalling to contemplate, but she was becoming helpless and useless in our service. She was shaken loose in every joint, at least she seemed so; the brass on her journals and boxes was melted by the heat; her great steel tires almost red hot, while she smoked and sizzled at every joint. Our race was almost run.

CHAPTER III.

Run Down at Last—We Jump the Train and Fly to the Woods under Musketry Fire—How the Chase was Made—The Obstacles We Had to Encounter—Sensational Rebel Account of the Whole Affair—The Confederacy Badly "Shook Up."

A FEW minutes before we came to our final halt, Andrews, Brown, Knight and myself, who were on the engine and tender, having given up all hope of success, hastily discussed as to the best thing to be done, and it was concluded that the best course was to separate and scatter in all directions. In this way some of the party might possibly get away, while if we went in a body and continued together, with the great number of rebel troops in our front and in the rear, and, in fact, on all sides of us, the capture of the entire party would be absolutely certain. In accordance with this conclusion, Andrews now told us all that it was "every man for himself;" that we must scatter and do the best we could to escape to the Federal lines. We put down the brakes and as we sprang off and she stopped, her motion was reversed, with the hope that she would run back and either cause collision or delay to the on-rushing train, with its frenzied, bloodthirsty passengers behind us, thereby giving us a little lever—she would not budge a wheel nor move an inch, but stood useless and sullen on the track—she was dead.

We did not stop even to take a farewell look but all struck for the woods, scattering in all directions except behind us. They came thundering up to within two hundred yards of where we stopped, and we could hear them shout, "Halt!" "Halt!" and while some were leaping off the cars, others opened fire on us with their muskets. Between the shrill whistle and steam of their locomotive, their infernal screeches and yells and the musketry fire, it seemed as if all Bedlam had been turned loose. This tumult only lent wings to our flight. The musket balls began to fly uncomfortably thick; but we only ran the faster. As I jumped and ran from the train I heard my name called, and looking back, saw my comrade, Mark Wood, hastening after me. Halting for him we continued our flight together, and remained close companions in many an after-adventure in Dixie.

The reader may here be inclined to wonder, that with the start we had, the terrific speed with which we almost flew over the track, the rails we had torn up and the obstacles we had thrown out to impede our pursuers, why it was that they gained upon us so rapidly in such an incredibly short time. But it must be remembered that much valuable time was lost in passing down trains, at one place having waited twenty-five minutes for a train. Train after train passed us, and on one occasion as many as eight or ten locomotives in a string—cars both empty and loaded, all hurrying down the road in the effort to get all the available rolling stock and property to a place of safety from the clutches of General Mitchell's triumphant and advanc-

JUMPING FROM THE ENGINE.

ing army. Then, too, the time lost in getting wood and water, in cutting telegraph wires, altogether consumed many precious moments. The very excitement of the chase also brought those living near the track to the road in crowds, and they undoubtedly assisted in clearing obstructions as speedily as possible. The rebel account of the pursuit, published in the *Southern Confederacy,* at Atlanta, April 15, 1862, shows clearly how our pursuers gave us such a successful chase, and also shows the immense importance the Confederates attached to this reckless expedition, if it had been successful. I take the liberty here of reproducing the published account as it appeared in that paper, three days after the occurrence. It is as follows:

THE GREAT RAILROAD CHASE.

THE MOST EXTRAORDINARY AND ASTOUNDING ADVENTURE OF THE WAR—THE MOST DARING UNDERTAKING THAT YANKEES EVER PLANNED OR ATTEMPTED TO EXECUTE—STEALING AN ENGINE—TEARING UP THE TRACK—PURSUED ON FOOT, ON HAND-CARS, AND ENGINES—OVERTAKEN—A SCATTERING—THE CAPTURE—THE WONDERFUL ENERGY OF MESSRS. FULLER, MURPHY AND CAIN—SOME REFLECTIONS, ETC. , ETC.

Since our last issue we have obtained full particulars of the most thrilling railroad adventure that ever occurred on the American Continent, as well as the mightiest and most important in its results, if successful, that has been conceived by the Lincoln Government since the commencement of this war. Nothing on so grand a scale has been attempted, and nothing within the range of possibility could be conceived that would fall with such a tremendous crushing force upon us, as the accomplishment of the plans which were concocted and dependent on the execution of the one whose history we now proceed to narrate.

Its reality—what was actually done—excels all the extravagant *conceptions* of the Arrow-Smith hoax, which fiction created such a profound sensation in Europe.

To make the matter more complete and intelligible, we will take our readers over the same history of the case which we related in our last, the main features of which are correct, but are lacking in details, which have since come to hand.

We will begin at the breakfast table of the Big Shanty Hotel, at Camp McDonald, on the W. & A. R. R., where several regiments of soldiers are now encamped. The morning mail and passenger train had left here at 4 A. M. on last Saturday morning as usual, and had stopped there for breakfast. The conductor, William A. Fuller, the engineer, I. Cain—both of this city—and the passengers were at the table, when some eight men, having uncoupled the engine and three empty box-cars next to it from the passenger and baggage cars, mounted the engine, pulled open the valve, put on all steam, and left conductor, engineer, passengers, spectators, and the soldiers in the camp hard by, all lost in amazement and dumbfounded at the strange, startling and daring act.

This unheard-of act was doubtless undertaken at that place and time, upon the presumption that pursuit could not be made by an engine short of Kingston, some thirty miles above, or from this place; and that by cutting down the telegraph wires as they proceeded, the adventurers could calculate on at least three or four hours the start of any pursuit it was reasonable to expect. This was a legitimate conclusion, and but for the will, energy and quick good judgment of Mr. Fuller and Mr. Cain, and Mr. Anthony Murphy, the intelligent and practical foreman of the wood department of the State road shop, who accidentally went on the train from this place that morning, their calculations would have worked out as originally contemplated, and the results would have been obtained long ere this reaches the eyes of our readers—the most terrible to us of any that we can conceive as possible, and unequaled by anything attempted or conceived since this war commenced.

Now for the chase!

These three determined men, without a moment's delay, put out after the flying train—*on foot,* amidst shouts of laughter by the crowd, who, though lost in amazement at the unexpected and daring act, could not repress their risibility at seeing three men start after a train on foot, which they had just witnessed depart at lightning speed. They put on all their speed, and ran along the track for three miles, when they came across some track-raisers, who had a small truck-car, which is shoved along by men so employed on railroads, on which to carry their tools. This truck and men were at once "impressed" They took it by turns of two at a time to run behind this truck and push it along all up grades and level portions of the road, and let it drive at will on all the down grades. A little way further up the fugitive adventurers had stopped, cut the telegraph wires and torn up the track. Here the pursuers were thrown off pell-mell, truck and men, upon the side of the road. Fortunately, "nobody was hurt on our side." The truck was soon placed on the road again; enough hands were left to repair the track and with all the power of determined will and muscle, they pushed on to Etowah Station, some twenty miles above.

Here, most fortunately, Major Cooper's old coal engine, the "Yonah"—one of the first engines on the State road—was standing out, fired up. This venerable locomotive was immediately turned upon her old track and like an old racer at the tap of the drum, pricked up her ears and made fine time to Kingston.

The fugitives, not expecting such early pursuit, quietly took in wood and water at Cass Station, and borrowed a schedule from the tank-tender upon the plausible plea that they were running a pressed train, loaded with powder for Beauregard. The attentive and patriotic tank-tender, Mr. William Russell, said he gave them his schedule, and would have sent the shirt off his back to Beauregard, if it had been asked for. Here the adventurous fugitives inquired which end of the switch they should go in on at Kingston. When they arrived at Kingston, they stopped, went to the agent there, told the powder story, readily got the switch-key, went on the upper turn-out, and waited for the down *way freight train to pass.* To all inquiries they replied with the same powder story. When the freight train had passed, they immediately proceeded on to the next station—Adairsville—where they were to meet the *regular down freight train.* At some point on the way they had taken on some fifty cross-ties, and before reaching Adairsville. they stopped on a curve, tore up the rails, and put several cross-ties on the track—no doubt intending to wreck this down freight train, which would be along in a few minutes. They had out upon the engine a red handkerchief, as a kind of flag or signal, which, in railroading, means another train is behind—thereby indicating to all that the regular passenger train would be along presently. They stopped a moment at Adairsville, and said Fuller, with the regular passenger train, was behind, and would wait at Kingston for the freight train, and told the conductor thereon to push ahead and meet him at that point. They passed on to Calhoun, where they met the down passenger train, due here at 4:20 P.M., and without making any stop, they proceeded—on, on and on.

But we must return to Fuller and his party whom we have unconsciously left on the old "Yonah" making their way to Kingston.

Arriving there and learning the adventurers were but twenty minutes ahead, they left the "Yonah" to blow off, while they mounted the engine of the Rome Branch Road, which was ready fired up and waiting for the arrival of the passenger train nearly due, when it would have proceeded to Rome. A large party of gentlemen volunteered for the chase, some at Acworth, Allatoona, Kingston and other points, taking such arms as they could lay their hands on at the moment; and with this fresh engine they set out with all speed but with great "care and caution," as they had scarcely time to make Adairsville before the down freight train would leave that point. Sure enough, they discovered this side of Adairsville three rails torn up and other impediments in the way. They "took up" in time to prevent an accident, but could proceed with the train no further. This was most vexatious, and it may have been in some degree disheartening, but it did not cause the slightest relaxation of efforts, and as the result proved was but little in the way of the *dead game,* pluck and resolutions of Fuller and Murphy, who left the engine and again *put out on foot alone!* After running two miles they met the down freight train, one mile out from Adairsville. They immediately reversed the train and run backwards to Adairsville—put the cars on the siding and pressed forward, making fine time to Calhoun, where they met the regular down passenger train. Here they halted a moment, took on board a telegraph operator, and a number of men who again volunteered, taking their guns along—and continued the chase. Mr. Fuller also took on here a company of track hands to repair the track as they went along. A short distance above Calhoun they *flushed their game* on a curve, where they doubtless supposed themselves out of danger, and were quietly oiling the engine, taking up the track, etc. Discovering that they were pursued, they mounted and sped away, throwing out upon the track as they went along the heavy cross-ties they had prepared themselves with. This was done by breaking out the end of the hindmost box-car, and pitching them out. Thus, "nip and tuck," they passed with fearful speed Resaca, Tilton, and on through Dalton.

The rails which they had taken up last they took off with them—besides throwing out cross-ties upon the track occasionally—hoping thereby the more surely to impede the pursuit; but all this was like tow to the touch of fire, to the now thoroughly aroused, excited and eager pursuers. These men, though so much excited and influenced by so much determination, still retained their well-known caution, were looking out for this danger and discovered it, and though it was seemingly an insuperable obstacle to their making any headway in pursuit, was quickly overcome by the genius of Fuller and Murphy. Coming to where the rails were torn up, they stopped, tore up rails behind them, and laid them down before, till they passed over that obstacle. When the cross-ties were reached, they hauled to and threw them off, and thus proceeded, and under these difficulties gained on the fugitives. At Dalton they halted a moment. Fuller put off the telegraph operator, with instructions to telegraph to Chattanooga to have them stopped, in case he should fail to overhaul them.

Fuller pressed on in hot chase—sometimes in sight—as much to prevent their cutting the wires before the message could be sent as to catch them. The daring adventurers stopped just opposite and very near to where Colonel Glenn's regiment is encamped, and cut the wires, but the operator at Dalton *had put the message through about two minutes before.* They also again tore up the track, cut down a telegraph-pole, and placed the two ends under the cross-ties, and the middle over the rail on the track. The pursuers stopped again and got over this impediment in the same manner they did before—taking up rails behind and laying them down before. Once over this, they shot on, and passed through the great tunnel, at Tunnel Hill, being then only five minutes behind. The fugitives thus finding themselves closely pursued, uncoupled two of the box-cars from the engine, to impede the progress of the pursuers. Fuller hastily coupled them to the front of his engine, and pushed them ahead of him to the first turn-out or siding, where they were left—thus preventing the collision the adventurers intended.

Thus the engine-thieves passed Ringgold, where they began to fag. They were out of wood, water and oil. Their rapid running and inattention to the engine, had melted all the brass from the journals. They had no time to repair or refit, for an iron horse of more bottom was close behind. Fuller and Murphy and their men soon came within four hundred yards of them, when the fugitives jumped from the engine and left it—three on the north side and five on the south side—all fleeing precipitately and scattering through the thicket. Fuller and his party also took to the woods after them.

Some gentlemen, also well armed, took the engine and some cars of the down passenger train at Calhoun, and followed up Fuller and Murphy and their party in the chase, but a short distance behind, and reached the place of the stampede but a very few moments after the first pursuers did. A large number of men were soon mounted, armed, and scouring the country in search of them. Fortunately there was a militia muster at Ringgold. A great many countrymen were in town. Hearing of the chase, they put out on foot and on horseback, in every direction, in search of the daring, but now thoroughly frightened and fugitive men.

We learn that Fuller, soon after leaving his engine, in passing a cabin in the country, found a mule having on a bridle but no saddle, and tied to a fence. "*Here's your mule,*" he shouted, as be leaped upon his back and put out as fast as a good switch, well applied, could impart vigor to the muscles and accelerate the speed of the patient donkey. The cry of "Here's your mule!" and "Where's my mule?" have become national, and are generally heard when, on the one hand, no mule is about, and on the other, when no one is hunting a mule. It seems not to be understood by any one, though it is a peculiar Confederate phrase, and is as popular as "Dixie" from the Potomac to the Rio Grande. It remained for Fuller, in the midst of this exciting chase, to solve the mysterious meaning of this national bye-word or phrase, and give it a practical application.

All of the eight men were captured, and are now safely lodged in jail. The particulars of their capture we have not received. This we hope to obtain in time for a postscript to this, or for our second edition. They confessed that they belonged to Lincoln's army, and had been sent down from Shelbyville to burn the bridges between here and Chattanooga; and that the whole party consisted of nineteen men, eleven of whom were dropped at several points on the road as they came down, to assist in the burning of the bridges as they went back.

When the morning freight train which left this city reached Big Shanty, Lieutenant Colonels R. F. Maddox and C. P. Phillips took the engine and a few cars, with fifty picked men, well armed, and followed on as rapidly as possible. They passed over all difficulties, and got as far as Calhoun, where they learned the fugitives had taken to the woods, and were pursued by plenty of men, with the means to catch them if it were possible.

One gentleman, who went up on the train from Calhoun, who has furnished us with many of these particulars, and who, by the way, is one of the most experienced railroad men in Georgia, says too much praise cannot be bestowed on Fuller and Murphy, who showed a cool judgment and forethought in this extraordinary affair, unsurpassed by anything he ever knew in a railroad emergency. This gentleman, we learn from another, offered, on his own account, $100 reward on each man, for the apprehension of the villains.

We do not know what Governor Brown will do in this case, or what is his custom in such matters, but if such a thing is admissable, we insist on Fuller and Murphy being promoted to the highest honors on the road—if not by actually giving them the highest positions, at least let them be promoted by *brevet.* Certainly their indomitable energy and quick, correct judgment and decision in the many difficult contingencies connected with this unheard of emergency, has saved all the railroad bridges above Ringgold from being burned; the most daring scheme that this revolution has developed has been thwarted, and the tremendous results which, if successful, can scarcely be imagined, much less described, have been averted. Had they succeeded in burning the bridges, the enemy at Huntsville would have occupied Chattanooga before Sunday night. Yesterday they would have been in Knoxville, and thus had possession of all East Tennessee. Our forces at Knoxville, Greenville and Cumberland Gap would, ere this, have been in the hands of the enemy. Lynchburgh, Va., would have been moved upon at once. This would have given them possession of the valley of Virginia and Stonewall Jackson could have been attacked in the rear. They would have possession of the railroad leading to Charlottesville and Orange Court House, as well as the South Side Railroad, leading to Petersburgh and Richmond. They might have been able to unite with McClellan's forces and attack Jo. Johnston's army, front and flank. It is not by any means improbable that our army in Virginia would have been defeated, captured or driven out of the State this week.

Then reinforcements from all the Eastern and Southeastern portion of the country would have been cut off from Beauregard. The enemy have Huntsville now, and with all these designs accomplished his army would have been effectually flanked. The mind and heart shrink appalled at the awful consequences that would have followed the success of this one act. When Fuller, Murphy and Cain started from Big Shanty *on foot to capture that fugitive engine,* they were involuntarily laughed at by the crowd, serious as the matter was—and to most observers it was indeed most ludicrous; but *that foot race saved us*, and prevented the consummation of all these tremendous consequences.

One fact, we must not omit to mention, is the valuable assistance rendered by Peter Bracken, the engineer on the down freight train which Fuller and Murphy turned back. He ran his engine fifty and a half miles—two of them backing the whole freight train up to Adairsville—made twelve stops, coupled to the two cars which the fugitives had dropped, and switched them off on sidings—all this, *in one hour and five minutes.*

We doubt if the victory of Manassas or Corinth were worth as much to us as the frustration of this grand *coup d' etat.* It is not by any means certain that the annihilation of Beauregard's whole army at Corinth would be so fatal a blow to us as would have been the burning of the bridges at that time and by these men.

When we learned by a private telegraph dispatch a few days ago, that the Yankees had taken Huntsville, we attached no great importance to it. We regarded it merely as a dashing foray of a small party to destroy property, tear up the road, etc., *a la* Morgan. When an additional telegram announced the Federal force there to be from seventeen thousand to twenty thousand, we were inclined to doubt—though coming from a perfectly honorable and upright gentleman, who would not be apt to seize upon a wild report to send here to his friends. The coming to that point with a large force, where they would be flanked on either side by our army, we regarded as a most stupid and unmilitary act. We now understand it all. They were to move upon Chattanooga and Knoxville as soon as the bridges were burnt, and press on into Virginia as far as possible, and take all our forces in that State in the rear. It was all the deepest laid scheme and on the grandest scale that ever emanated from the brains of any number of Yankees combined. It was one that was also, entirely practicable on almost any day for the last year. There were but two miscalculations in the whole programme; they did not expect men to start on foot to pursue them, and they did not expect these pursuers on foot to find Major Cooper's old "Yonah" standing there all ready fired up. Their calculations on every other point were dead certainties, and would have succeeded perfectly.

This would have eclipsed anything Captain Morgan ever attempted. To think of a parcel of Federal soldiers, officers and privates, coming down into the heart of the Confederate States—for they were here in Atlanta and at Marietta—(some of them got on the train at Marietta that morning and others were at Big Shanty;) of playing such a serious game on the State Road, which is under the control of our prompt, energetic and sagacious Governor, known as such all over America; to seize the passenger train on his road, right at Camp McDonald, where he has a number of Georgia regiments encamped, and run off with it; to burn the bridges on the same road, and go safely through to the Federal lines—all this would have been a feather in the cap of the man or men who executed it.

Let this be a warning to the railroad men and every body else in the Confederate States. Let an engine never be left alone a moment. Let additional guards be placed at our bridges. This is a matter we specially urged in the Confederacy long ago. We hope it will now be heeded. Further: let a sufficient guard be placed to watch the government stores in this city; and let increased vigilance and watchfulness be put forth by the watchmen. We know one solitary man who is guarding a house in this city, which contains a lot of bacon. Two or three men could throttle and gag him and set fire to the house at any time; and worse, he conceives that there is no necessity for a guard, as he is sometimes seen off duty, for a few moments—fully long enough for an incendiary to burn the house he watches. Let Mr. Shakelford, whom we know to be watchful and attentive to his duties, take the responsibility at once of placing a well armed guard of sufficient force around every house containing government stores. Let this be done without waiting for instructions from Richmond.

One other thought. The press is required by the Government to keep silent about the movements of the army, and a great many things of the greatest interest to our people. It has, in the main, patriotically complied. We have complied in most cases, but our judgment was against it all the while. The plea is that the enemy will get the news, if it is published in our papers. Now, we again ask, what's the use? The enemy get what information they want. They are with us and pass among us almost daily. They find out from us what they want to know, by passing through our country unimpeded. It is nonsense, it is folly, to deprive our own people of knowledge they are entitled to and ought to know, for fear the enemy will find it out. We ought to have a regular system of passports over all our roads, and refuse to let any man pass who could not give a good account of himself—come well vouched for and make it fully appear that he is not an enemy, and that he is on legitimate business. This would keep information from the enemy far more effectually than any reticence of the press, which ought to lay before our people the full facts in everything of a public nature.

CHAPTER IV.

"Nip and Tuck"—A Grand Old "Yankee" Man-Hunt—Citizen, Soldiers and Dogs Join the Chase—Mark Wood and I Squat in a Little Brush Pile—The Secesh Come to the Hunt by Hundreds—"Ticklish" Situation for Thirty-Six Hours—Escape to the Mountains—Discovered by Women in a Fodder-Pile—We Tell a Plausible Story—Begging Victuals—Another Lynx-Eyed Woman—"You Are Union Men; You Can't Fool Me."

"By night I heard them on the track,
Their troops came hard upon our back,
With their long gallop, which can tire
The hound's deep hate, and hunter's fire."

To return to our flight from the engine. After running some distance, Wood and I came to a large, open field, on the slope of a mountain just in front of us. To attempt to cross this wide, open space would expose us too much for safety, besides, we were nearly out of breath—too near, at least, to attempt such a run. We were in much perplexity as to what to do. We could hear the enemy shouting, and the constant report of fire-arms warned us that the remorseless, blood-thirsty crowd was waging a war of extermination, and, as we listened, we could distinctly hear them coming as well as see them. There was no time to be lost. A fortuitous circumstance saved us. The woods were too open for a man to hide in, but as I glanced about I saw where a tree had been cut down, probably in the summer previous, and the brush which had been trimmed off lay scattered around with the dried leaves still clinging to it. My plan was formed instantly and I told Wood to lay down. I hastily laid a few leafy boughs on him in such a manner as not to show that they had been displaced. Mark was soon out of sight in a little flat, unpretentious pile, that would scarcely be noticed among the other rubbish, and with almost the quickness of a rabbit I slipped out of sight under the heap by Mark's side. I now drew my revolver and told Mark to do likewise. I felt a sense of desperation which I had never felt before. We were in a high state of excitement and realized that the frenzied crowd of man-hunters, then deploying all over the woods, would show us no mercy. From the constant report of fire-arms which rang in our ears, we had reason to believe that some of our unfortunate comrades were being shot down like cattle, perhaps all except ourselves had been killed. We felt that in all human probability we would be discovered, indeed it seemed almost impossible that they could miss finding us. We felt that if discovered it would be more manly to stand up and die fighting, even against great odds and with no hope of escape, than to be shot down like dogs unresistingly, or, in the alternative that we should possibly be taken prisoners, hung like felons, at the end of a sham trial.

We were surrounded on every side by enemies thirsting for our blood. As I afterwards learned, within a few hundred yards from where we left our engine, two regiments of cavalry were encamped. It was muster-day at Ringgold, two miles away, and hundreds of farmers, armed and mounted, were collected there. The road was lined with soldiers. The alarm had been sent to Chattanooga by telegraph, and trains loaded with troops and scouts were hurrying to the scene. The day was dark, cloudy and rainy. Our boys were unacquainted with the country, and with the stars and sun hidden did not know the south from the north. Within an hour or two the whole country was alive with scouts and hunters. There was not a by-path or cross-road that was not thoroughly explored. To add to the terrors of the situation, well-trained hounds were put upon the track of our party, and many of them were trailed down with unerring certainty. In my concealment I felt all the desperation and anguish of mind that a man could feel in my situation. We had failed and were disappointed. We had been run down and had gone to the last extremity of human endurance to make our escape. Our enemies were infuriated. We had made such superhuman exertions within the last half hour, ending in our up-hill race to the brush-heap, that we were almost breathless. It did not at that time seem to me that it would require many rebel bullets to finish my part of the story. Several times, as they passed us so close that I could have touched their legs with my hand, I was on the point of springing up, and, with a loud yell, beginning the work of death at close range with my revolver. I could not, even in a whisper, communicate my wishes to Wood, without betraying our place of concealment. Our hearts thumped so loud that it seemed to me they could be heard twenty-yards distant. Mark had run till he could run no further. But our pursuers made so much noise themselves that they could hear nothing else. They were all yelling, swearing, cursing and shooting. They were like dogs chasing a rabbit in tall weeds—all jumping and looking high, while the *game* was close to the ground. We could hear much of the conversation as they passed us. Two stalwart johnnies, each with a musket, as they passed near us, spied two of our comrades going across a distant part of the great open field.

"There goes two of them," said one of the johnnies. "Come on, let's go for them!"

"Let us get some more help," said the other.

"But, you see, they have no guns," said the first.

And thus they passed out of hearing, halting and debating, but evidently distrusting the policy of tackling the train-robbers even-handed.

It was some time in the afternoon when we took refuge in the brush-heap, and in that spot we were compelled to remain all that night, all the next day and far into the second night, before we dared venture forth. The night was one of terrible anxiety to us. Our condition was perilous in the extreme. The entire night long could be heard the shouts and yells and imprecations and firing of the frenzied horde. The whole country was aroused and swarmed with soldiers and citizens. Every road and cross-road was watched night and day that none of the "rascals" might escape. We could hear the deep baying of blood-hounds, as they scoured through woods and fields, but, luckily for us, so many men had tramped over the ground in the vicinity of the place where we jumped from the train that the dogs could not work. Still men and dogs were scouring the woods in every direction and it was unsafe to make *tracks*. To add still more to the wretchedness of our condition, the rain was almost incessant. The place of our concealment was a little lower than the ground surrounding and much of the time the water was three or four inches deep where we lay. This, with hunger and wet clothing, made us extremely uncomfortable.

After darkness had closed in for some time, on the second night, however, we were compelled to come out, capture or no capture. We could stand it no longer. On crawling out, our limbs were so stiff and sore that it was with the utmost difficulty that we could move, and it was only by rubbing and working them vigorously that we could begin to use them. It did not seem that we could travel very far, do our best, with such stiffened limbs. After looking about, we decided to take an opposite course from that which our comrades had taken, thinking there would be less vigilance on the part of the hunters in that direction. We desired also to get into the mountains, thinking we would there have a better chance for our lives. I suppose at this time we were less than twenty miles from Chattanooga. The rain still fell in torrents, but as we went on and our stiffened limbs got limbered up, we began to make good time. Our desire was, as soon as we could get beyond the immediate reach of our enemies, to bend our course in the direction of the Federal lines. But we must by all means avoid Chattanooga. We know that.

We traveled as rapidly as we could that night, and about daybreak, of Monday morning, we saw an old log hut off by itself some distance from any road. We wished very much to get shelter from the cold rain, which had chilled us almost to the point of freezing. We found the hut to be a sort of barn, the mow of which was full of bundles of corn-fodder. We made a hole down in the mow and covered ourselves out of sight and went to sleep.

About one o'clock in the day, as we slumbered, we were awakened by somebody in the mow and soon found out that two women were looking there for eggs. One of them nearest us said: "Here is a hole; I wouldn't wonder if there is a nest in here;" and at the same time she thrust her hand down and, as bad luck would have it she touched one of my hands and started back with a scream, which brought up the other woman and they threw off the bundles and there we were. They were both badly frightened and ran for the house with all their might. We hastily crawled out and brushed some of the chaff from our clothes and after a moment's thought concluded that the best thing for us to do would be to go to the house and apologize to them and in addition try to get something to eat.

Who is the man who has ever in his life vainly appealed, in a becoming and respectful manner, for food, when hungry, to a woman? If man excels in the brutal art of war and killing his fellow beings with successful and unsparing hand, or being himself killed without a murmer, all of which passes for bravery, noble woman excels in those higher and more Godlike attributes of sympathy for the distressed and charity to the needy. I believe this to be true the world over, where woman is treated as the equal of man.

We went to the door, bowed politely and apologized for the unintentional scare we had caused them. We then told them we had been in pursuit of the train-robbers and that wet, cold and sleepy, we preferred to take shelter in the barn rather than disturb any one at the dead hour of night. This story seemed to be satisfactory to them, when we told them we were hungry and asked them for something to eat. They had just had their dinner and the table still stood out on the floor. They gave us a pitcher of butter milk and some corn-bread, all they had unless we would wait for them to cook us something, which we did not wish them to do, as we did not care to make our visit too tedious. This was the first food we had eaten since the morning we left Marietta and homely as was the fare it tasted good. We paid them and left much refreshed and strengthened by our food and rest. We started away on a road, but as soon as we got well out of sight of the house we changed our course and soon after concealed ourselves in a dense thicket and there awaited the shades of night to come and conceal our further movements.

We had not been in the thicket long before we saw a squad of mounted soldiers pass down the road we had previously left and which was some distance from us. From their loud talk and their manner of march, we concluded they were a party of man-hunters. Whether they had gained any information at the house where we had been we could not tell, but we laid down and kept quiet. When night came we shaped our course as near as we could, without following any road, toward the Tennessee River, east of Chattanooga. During the night march we narrowly missed running into a guard post at the crossing of a road, but fortunately heard them in time. We went around them and on our way undisturbed. At the dawn of Tuesday we had just arrived at the foot of the mountains and breathed easier, for we felt more secure than we had in the open country. We concealed ourselves in a comfortable place and witnessed the rising of the sun. Its loveliness and genial warmth never before cheered me so much as then. But we soon fell asleep from weariness and did not wake until nearly night. As soon as it was dark we started again. We had a toilsome night march, feeling our way over rocks, climbing precipitous places and at other times descending the steep mountain side on the run, through bushes and among rocks.

When Wednesday morning came we found that we were still surrounded by mountains on all sides, with no signs of a habitation or a human being in sight. When the sun got well up and it was comfortably warm, we lay down and took a nap. The pangs of hunger were, by this time, pressing us distressingly. We had in all this time only tasted food once since the raid began and that was the scanty meal we made on buttermilk and corn-bread, Monday afternoon. In this starving extremity we decided that there was no great risk run in this lonely region if we should travel by day, and after so deciding, we pushed on with our utmost energy, as a hungry man will do when he hopes soon to find food.

We were guiding our course by the sun, and during the afternoon we came out on the brow of a high mountain, overlooking a beautiful little valley, thickly dotted with houses. From our elevated position we could see everything the valley contained. I thought it one of the loveliest sights I had ever seen—that quiet, peaceful little valley. I looked at each house and wished that I could go into even the humblest and ask for a piece of corn-bread. I pictured in my hungry imagination the good things to eat in each little cottage, and wondered how we could safely manage to get a morsel of their stores of abundance to satisfy our great hunger. The more I looked at that little valley the more it looked like a little paradise of peace and plenty, where sorrow and hunger never entered. And the longer I looked, the hungrier I became.

Near the foot of the mountain was a small log house, a little separated from the rest, and we knew it was inhabited from the smoke that curled up from the chimney. We concluded to venture down and apply for food. A young-looking woman appeared at the door, and, after the salutations of the day, we told her that we had been lost in the mountains and were in need of something to eat. She invited us to seats, and at once set about getting us a meal. We inquired the way to the next town, the name of which I pretended I could not just speak, but she helped me out by mentioning the name—Cleveland. We learned from her that the town was only a short distance away and that there were no soldiers there. This was gratifying, but not near as much so as the savory odors of the ham, eggs and rye coffee she was preparing for us. We could hardly wait until the corn-bread was cooked, and when she invited us to take seats at her table, we soon gave her satisfactory evidence that we had told the truth about being hungry, although we had stretched the facts a little about being lost. We paid the woman for our dinner, and, without delay, took our leave.

We felt very much the need of a map, and after a near approach to the little town of Cleveland, and a careful survey of the surroundings, I left Wood in a secluded spot to wait while I walked boldly in and went to a book-store and asked for a school atlas. They had Mitchell's Geography and Atlas. As the author was none other than my commanding General, I had no reason to doubt that through the aid of his map I might reach his camp, if he had not moved too far since I left. I had to buy the geography too if I took the atlas, and, taking the books under my arm, like some countryman who lived near by in the mountains, no one seemed to pay any attention to me. We were soon in the woods again, when we tore out such portions of the atlas as we needed and hid the rest under a log, after which we took our course and pushed on, making good progress. We knew that we must, by this time, be in the vicinity of the Tennessee River. Our plan was to reach the river as soon as possible and secure a boat of some kind, after which we would drift down the river to Bridgeport, Stevenson, or some point nearest the Federal lines.

Towards evening of this day we came to the terminus of the mountain in this direction, and from its great height we had a commanding view of the valley below, which, though beautiful in scenery, was sparsely settled. In the evening we descended, the mountain and felt our way cautiously across the valley. After a time we came to a log house. There seemed to be no stir about the premises, and, as we were still hungry, we concluded to apply for something more to eat. We had been so hungry that we had not dared to eat all our appetites craved at the last place.

There was no man to be seen about the house, but the woman, who was a noble, dignified-looking lady, plainly dressed, told us to be seated. I noticed her looking at us with that scrutinizing, inquiring gaze of a woman in doubt, and I could read her thoughts as plainly as if she had spoken them to us. I knew enough about woman, too, to know that whatever her first impressions are they would be unchangeable, so I said, without further hesitation, "We are in need of something to eat." She said if we could put up with such fare as she had we were welcome. We told her that we were quite hungry and any kind of food would be welcome. As she proceeded about her work, I noticed that on every opportunity she scrutinized us very sharply, and I became a little uneasy.

Presently she asked us if we were traveling, to which I replied that we were on our way to Harrison, which was a small village a few miles from there. I still noticed that she was eyeing us keenly and closely, and that her mind was not at rest on the subject, when suddenly she turned, looked us squarely in the face and startled us by saying:

"You are Union men! You can't fool me! I know a Union man by his look. You need not deny it, nor need you be afraid to own it, either. I am a Union woman, and I am not afraid to own it to anybody. The secessionists around here don't like me a bit, for I say just what I think of them, whether they like it or not. Further, I know that you are Union men trying to get to the Union army and you need not go to the trouble to deny it. I will do anything I can to help you."

We stoutly denied any such intention, and told her that we had been soldiers in the Confederate army. But that did no good. She seemed to have made up her mind, and no assertions of ours could change it. So we let her have it her own way and we had ours. Soon after her husband came in. He was rather a fine-looking fellow, with a frank, manly face.

When supper was over we offered this loyal woman pay, but she refused to take our money, saying that anything she could do for a Union man she would do with a glad heart and willing hands. She said she wished the Union army would come—she would give them everything she had before the rebels came in and robbed them.

As we took our leave, she told her husband to give us all the information that he could as to our route, "For," said she to him, "you know old Snow, with his company of cavalry, is in the neighborhood, and he will be upon them before they know it. He is watching every nook and road in the settlement to prevent Union men from getting away from the rebel conscription."

We felt, while in the presence of these good people, that we were with friends, although we did not think it prudent to show any sort of sympathy or undue friendship with their expressions of loyalty, and, though we did not show it, we felt much regret at parting from them, for we seldom met with their like. We were convinced they were true Union people.

CHAPTER V.

Captured by Old Snow's Cavalry—A Deceptive Story that Wins—A Terrible Risk—"Circumstances Alter Cases"—Released—Taking the Oath—A Red-Hot Rebel Lecture—Again in the Mountains—A Loyal Woman in the Case, and Her No Less Loyal Husband—Stowed Away in a Safe Hiding Place—"I Knew You Were Union Men all the Time"—Night March with a Guide—Stealing a Boat—Safe Arrival on the Tennessee River—Night of Terror on the Tennessee—Storm of Sleet and Hail—Almost Frozen—Sheltered in a Cabin—A New Story Invented.

THAT night we passed in the woods, and continued our journey Thursday morning. The valley through which our course lay was thickly inhabited, and we had observed the greatest possible precaution, as we supposed, in avoiding "old Snow's" cavalry. Our surprise was all the greater then, when, without the least warning, we heard the stern command:

"Halt there, you! Halt, or I will blow your brains out."

A hasty glance around failed to discover any safe chance of retreat. We were captured, and there was no course for us to pursue but to submit to the unpleasant inevitable. We involuntarily clenched our revolvers at the first warning of danger, but it was useless to open a fight with a large cavalry squad—the odds was too great. We would stand no show at all and we thought perhaps we *could,* by a little diplomacy, effect our release from these captors.

The captain of the squad seemed to be a pompous, and, according to his own account, a blood-thirsty warrior, for he said it was not his custom to take prisoners but to hang and shoot all who fell into his hands. He asked us a great many questions, including, of course, our place of residence and our names, all of which we answered very promptly, although I will not say truthfully, for truth we deemed "too great a pearl to cast before such swine." We told him we lived in Harrison, and gave him some names we had picked up, in which we must have struck him just right, for at once he inquired after the "old men, our fathers," whom he said he knew. We told him they were in excellent health. He said he was glad to hear it for he was well acquainted with both of them. "But," he continued, looking at us very sternly, "boys, it's my impression that you are running away from the conscription and you deserve to be shot as traitors for wanting to join the d—d Yankees." We told him we had not the slightest intention of enlisting in the infernal. Yankee army, which was fast ruining the South and its people. After a moment's silence, and looking at us steadily, during which time, no doubt, he was mentally debating what course to pursue, he said:

"For all know you may belong to those spies and bridge-burners, and if I did not know your folks I would send you to Chattanooga, under arrest; but I will tell you what I will do: if you will take the oath and promise to go back home and stay until I call for you,

"HALT THERE, YOU"

I will allow you to do so. I have known both your fathers for many years and have great respect for them. They have always been true men to the South, and out of consideration for them I will permit you to go back on the conditions I have named.

Now, there may be those with a nice discrimination of conscience who will condemn me and my comrade in misfortune—who has long since ceased his struggle with the cold charities of the world which brought with all its joys many sorrows on the poor fellow's head for what we did—and if they do I shall not complain. But, dear comrade, or reader, I pray you before you lightly pass sentence of condemnation, remember that "circumstances alter cases." We were spies in citizens' clothes, inside the enemy's lines, caught near the camp—in one sense, liable to conviction under the rules of war, for prowling around the enemy's camp. Besides, we had committed a crime for which, if we were discovered, no mercy would be shown us. The professional detective or spy lives a life of constant deception. He professes to be what he is not. He practices deception to cover his tracks and to gain information, which cannot be had in a legitimate manner. Whether great exigencies of a public nature justify the practices necessary to the successful pursuit of such a profession, may be a question on which moral philosophers can well disagree, but which I am not competent to discuss.

But we were in no condition, for hair-splitting on minor points. Conscience, where the moral perceptions are to be consulted, and conscience, where a fellow's neck is at stake, are two different things. We were not professional spies or detectives, although, for the time being and for the good of the cause in which we enlisted, we were to all intents and purposes practicing the arts of a spy. Our game had been a desperate one from the start. The players on the other side were as desperate as we were. The stakes on our part were to save our necks from the halter—from the death of felons.

We had told a plausible story to this officer, by which we had so completely deceived him that he proposed to let us go, conditionally. He had named the conditions and for us to have rejected them would have refuted the statements we had just made to him, namely, that we were Confederates. Besides this, our detention a single hour might betray the falsity of our story about our living at Harrison. We were liable to be exposed any moment by some of the new troopers who were constantly arriving. We had to make our decision, and, quickly, too; hesitation would betray us. Wood and I cast hasty glances at each other. Nothing was said, but each seemed to read and understand the other's thoughts, which ran about to the effect. "it's the best thing we can do." We accordingly signified our acceptance of his conditions, and he at once ordered us to follow him, he leading us back to what proved to be the house of a rank old rebel and within a half mile of the house we had left the evening before. Here he went through the ceremony of what he termed administering the oath, after which he, with the aid of the hot tempered, forked-tongued old woman of the house, gave us the most fiery lecture on the subject of Southern rights and Northern wrongs we had ever heard. It was a one-sided affair, however, for we listened in silence, except now and then to put in a word as a clincher to some red-hot assertion they made. After the captain and old woman had both exhausted their vocabulary of words pretty well, we told the captain that we hoped it would not be long until he would find it convenient to call upon us for our services in the cause. He seemed much pleased at the favorable effect his eloquent harangue had worked upon us and as we hastily shook hands with him preparatory to leaving, he handed us back our revolvers, which he had previously taken from us.

This we considered a lucky escape and we started off in fine spirits after the depressing uncertainty occasioned by this capture. It was not long until we were again in the mountains, where we soon after found a place of safety where we rested and slept till near night. After we awoke we talked over the situation. What we desired was to get across the wide, thickly-settled valley to the river and find a boat. How to do it and evade capture was what concerned us most just now. If, by a streak of bad luck, we should again fall into the hands of old Snow or his crowd, we would fare hard, for we had promised him to take the back track. In this state of perplexity we decided to trust ourselves in the hands of the man and woman who had treated us so kindly and professed so much devotion to the Union cause. We knew that if the man was true, as he professed to be, that he could render us the assistance we so much needed. We had reason to believe, too, that both he and his wife were just what they professed—truly loyal people to our cause. We knew however, that if we ventured near this house that we must do it with great caution, otherwise we might be discovered, and thus not only be captured, but compromise our good, kind friends.

It was, therefore, late on Thursday evening, when, having left Wood a few paces from the house to keep a look-out, I went noiselessly to the door and knocked. The family had retired and the house was still as death. I knocked again and again, but finally heard the woman tell her husband there was some one at the door. Soon the man opened the door and seemed to know me at the first glance or by the sound of my voice. He spoke to me kindly and invited me in. While he was speaking to me I observed from some indications, I could not distinctly see, that his wife stood near by to kill me instantly in case any sign of foul play had been noticed. Those were times in Tennessee and Northern Georgia, and other places in the South, when some shocking tragedies took place. Men were hunted and shot down in their own door-yards and homes, for their loyalty to the old flag, and these persecuted, hunted people were generally ready for the worst and generally defended themselves to the death. In this defense the women often took a ready hand. The woman I am now speaking of would have been a dangerous one for any rebel to have attacked, if she had been given the least warning or had half a chance. It need then be no matter of surprise that she held a cocked rifle on me as I stood near the door, ready, on the least suspicious movement on my part, to have dropped me in my tracks.

I told the man I would like to speak a few words with him privately. He stepped a few paces from the door so that we were sure no person was in hearing distance. I then, in a low tone of voice, asked him if he could, of his own free, voluntary will, assist a Union man in distress, if he had the opportunity. I then paused and watched him intently and at once noticed that he was embarrassed. He acted like a man who suspected some trick—as if he thought I had been sent to entrap him for the purpose of betraying his loyalty. I was assured by his actions; for had he been a rebel and had wished to entrap me, he would have unhesitatingly answered, "Yes," and encouraged me to reveal myself. I relieved his embarrassment by saying, "There is no trick in this; I am a Union man in deep trouble, the nature of which I am not just at liberty to mention now. I need a friend and assistance." He then answered and said he would render any assistance in his power, not only to us but for the Union cause.

Wood had by this time come to where we were and I told the stranger to hold up his hand and be sworn, which he did, and I administered to him the following oath:

"You do most solemnly swear in our presence and before ALMIGHTY GOD, that you will not betray us to our enemies, but that you will do all that lies in your power to secrete, aid, protect and defend us."

To all of which he answered, "I will."

We then shook hands, and after making sure that no ear could hear us, I revealed to him a part of our story and who we were. He was a brave man and a true man, and, hearing our story, seemed to increase his interest and friendship in our behalf. We watched this man closely to observe if he took such precautions as a man would take who honestly desired our safety, and were gratified to see that he did. About the first thing, he told us that we must not come near, nor be seen about his house. He told us to follow him, and he led the way to an old abandoned house, where he had first lived when he located on the farm, and which stood in a secluded spot, remote from the road. In the center of the old floor was a trap-door, which opened into a hole about four feet square, which, during the occupancy of the house, had been used as a sort of cellar. Here we took up our quarters. He then went to the house and brought out a bundle of quilts for us to lie on. He next told us to avoid talking loud, and keep out of sight, in which case we would be perfectly safe until he could get an opportunity to pilot us safely out. He told us that no human being would be apprised of our whereabouts, except his wife, who was our friend, and would do as much for our safety as himself. He then left us and went to the house, first telling us that he would visit us in the morning, and bring us rations. We fixed ourselves very comfortably with the quilts, and, although our bed-room would not admit of our stretching our limbs out full length, we doubled up and enjoyed a very comfortable night's rest, something we had not done before for a long time.

The next morning, Friday, we heard our friend not far off calling and feeding his pigs, and not long after he quietly lifted off a board over the little cellar, when we put out our heads, shook hands with him, and took a sniff of the morning air. He carried a small basket which seemed to contain corn, which he passed down to us, but we found our breakfast underneath the corn, and after taking it out we replaced the corn and gave him back the basket. He spoke a few encouraging words to us, telling us we must not get restive but bide our time, when he replaced the board, scattered some straw over the old floor and left us.

We had time and opportunity in this dark little den to deliberate on the follies of the past and build up hopes for the future. Our first and greatest anxiety was as to the fate of our comrades, from whom we had separated when we all jumped from the train. No one who has not been similarly situated can realize the anxious thoughts we had about them. We had lain near by and heard the rattle of musketry, the exultant shouts of the pursuers and the baying of the dogs in hot pursuit. It seemed impossible that all should escape. Perhaps we alone had been so fortunate. But who had been the unfortunate ones, and how had they met their fate? Perhaps some one more fortunate than the rest had by this time reached our comrades in the regiment and told them of the collapse of our expedition and that some of us were probably refugees in the mountains and our anxious friends at home would thus get some tidings from which to form conjectures as to our fate. These were some of the thoughts that occupied our minds in the dark, dismal little cellar. But thoughts of a still more weighty nature bore heavily upon us. They were of the present and near future.

While we were talking in a low tone of voice, we heard footsteps on the ground and soon after the board was lifted and some one spoke to us in a friendly voice. We put out our heads, and there stood before us, with the basket of corn, not our sworn friend of the night before, but his wife, the good, true Union, woman, to whom only a day or so before we had denied our country. It would be impossible for me to describe my feelings at that time in the presence of that noble, loyal, patriotic woman. I felt that we, men and soldiers as we were, had reason to feel humiliation in her presence for having doubted her word and her sincere professions of loyalty and friendship.

"I knew," said she, "that you were Union men all the time, and I am still ready to make good my promise, to not only do all I can for you, but for the Union cause." She told us that her husband had gone to assist a neighbor about some work and left us in her charge, and that she had brought our dinner. She spoke a few words of encouragement to us, and praised our daring effort, as she termed it, to steal the railroad away from the rebels, at the same time expressing her sorrow that we had not succeeded, and that the Union. army could not before that time have taken possession of the country and driven the rebels out. By this time we had taken our rations from the basket and replaced the corn, and she replaced the board over us and scattered straw about, as her husband had done, and left us.

In this way we remained secreted for several days. This delay was for several reasons. In the first place, we were nearly disabled with sore feet from our night marches in the mountains. In the next place, we knew that the longer the time that elapsed after the raid, the less vigilance would be observed by the rebels, who would tire of the pursuit. Then, most important of all, we had to wait till our friends could find a suitable person to conduct us out to the river safely, for the nights were, at that time, almost as light as day.

A trusty guide was found in the person of the brother of the loyal woman whose guests we then were. This young man, who knew the country well, conducted us by a circuitous night-march to a creek, perhaps the Chickamauga or McLarimore's, a tributary of the Tennessee.

Our great trouble had been, in this mountainous country, to keep the right course. Even if we knew the direction we desired to take, it was next to impossible to follow it by night travel, on account of the unevenness of the country. It was this that made us so anxious to reach the river, which would afford us a sure means of night travel, and guide us to a point near the Federal army. Unfortunately, when we reached the creek, the boat was on the opposite side.

Here our guide took his leave of us, and we set about finding a way to secure the boat. I first thought to swim the creek, which was very high and running driftwood. After considering the matter, however, I adopted a better plan. Mark secreted himself, near the bank below, where I could easily find him. I then went to an open space on the bank and halloed. It was now daylight, and a man soon answered. I told him I wished to cross over, and he soon came and took me to the other side. He was unable to change a five-dollar Confederate note, and I told him I expected to cross back next morning, and would try to have the change for him, which he said would do. I then walked briskly on the road leading to Harrison, until I came to the first turn in the road when I went into the woods and hid myself until dark. After dark I went back and cautiously approached the place where the boat was tied. After satisfying myself that the "coast was all clear," I hastily paddled over to the other side, took Mark aboard, and we were soon floating toward the Tennessee. After encountering some troublesome blockades of driftwood, and a rebel steamboat or patrol gunboat, we arrived safely in the Tennessee River.

This patrol boat gave us some concern. She lay in the mouth of the creek with her "nose" to the shore, while her stern lay not far from the opposite bank of the narrow stream. When we first saw her lights, we supposed it to be a cabin near the banks of the creek, and did not discover our mistake until we were right up to her, for the night was pitch dark, and it was raining. These latter circumstances enabled us, by lying down, and quietly steering our boat close under the stern of the steam craft, to glide by unnoticed. I thought if we only had our crowd of train boys along, and Wilson Brown to man the engine, we might easily have taken possession of the craft, and given the rebels another big scare, and, perhaps, all of us escape. But it might not have been any easier to steal a steamboat and get away with it than a railroad train. We drifted on, and in a few moments after, we were happy voyagers in the Tennessee River, going down stream with the swift current.

We felt this to be an achievement much in our favor. We had now a decidedly good chance of escape, if we observed due caution—at least we thought so. This night was one of the worst I ever remember of during my army life. Those comrades who have campaigned in East Tennessee, will not need be told how disagreeable a cold rain storm is there. The incessant rain was accompanied by a high wind, blinding our eyes much of the time, while the dark, rapid, seething waters carried our little boat on with maddening fury. Sometimes we would find ourselves going round and round in a great eddy or swirl, next striking the point of some island, or, nearly knocked from the boat by some low-hanging tree from a short turn in the river bank, or getting a startling thump from some on-rushing log or drifting tree. We were in constant apprehension, for in the black darkness, we could not see whither we were going, and so benumbed were we with wet and cold, that we had but little control of the boat, and our ears were our only guide for safety.

When the night was pretty well spent, we began to have a little anxiety as to where daylight would catch us. We knew we had been making good time, and that Chattanooga lay not far ahead of us. We also knew that it would not do for us to show ourselves in that locality in daylight. We now began to keep a look-out for a safe landing place. After several ineffectual attempts we found that to land along the steep banks, in our benumbed condition, was both difficult and dangerous. We soon discovered that we were passing what seemed to be a small island. We hugged close along the shore until we reached the lower end, and a place where the rapid current did not strike our boat, and by the aid of our paddles and the overhanging tree branches, we effected a safe landing in the dark, and drew our boat up on the bank. We took shelter under a great forked tree, and wrung the water from our coats.

The storm, by this time, had changed to sleet and hail, and it did seem to me that we must perish with cold. We beat our benumbed hands and arms about our bodies, to try to keep up the circulation of the blood, but we were chilled to the bone. I have never, not even in the coldest winter of the North, experienced so much suffering from cold as I did on that terrible night. Poor Wood, who afterwards died of consumption, seemed to suffer even more than I did. Never did I see the light of day approach with more gratitude than on that dismal island at the end of that night of terror. The sun brought no warmth, but its welcome light revealed to us a cabin near the shore, from whose stone chimney the smoke was curling up. We at once decided to go there and warm ourselves, even if we had to fight for the privilege, for we might as well perish fighting, as with the cold.

We at once launched our boat and crossed from the island to the shore. As we landed on the bank to go up to the house, Wood, whose teeth were chattering, and who looked both drowned and frozen, said to me, "Alf, you will have to make up some lie to tell them; they will ask us a thousand questions."

I said, "I don't know what I can tell them; I am too cold to speak the truth, though." But I told Mark to say but little, so that we need not "cross" one another in our story.

We were admitted to the cabin, and, as I stood before the great fire-place, I noticed the family viewing our bedraggled, drowned, forlorn appearance with some curiosity, especially the man of the house. After I got so that I could talk freely, I inquired if there were any boats about there. He said he knew of none except his own, which the Confederates allowed him to have to cross over to the island to his work. He then asked me if we were looking for boats. I told him we were, and that we had orders to destroy all we found, with the exception of a few owned and in charge of the right kind of men. I told him the object, of course, was to prevent Union men from running away from the conscription.

"I thought that was your business," said he. "There was a lot of soldiers along here a few days ago and destroyed every boat they could find."

He asked if we stayed at Chattanooga. I told him that our company was there. I further said: "Then you don't know of any boats along here, except your own?" He said he did not. After some further talk, I asked him if we could get some breakfast with them. He said we could. I then told him we were in the condition of most soldiers—that we had no money, but that I did not think it any dishonor for a man in the service of his country to ask for food. He said it was perfectly right.

We then took off our coats and hung them up to dry a little while we were at breakfast. After we had become thoroughly warmed, and partly dried our clothing, we took our leave, telling the man to keep an eye out for any boats that might possibly be lying about loose in his vicinity.

We now resumed our boat voyage, and did not spend much time hunting for strange boats, but availed ourselves of the first good opportunity to land and secrete ourselves. Our hiding place was in a thicket in a field, near enough where our boat was tied so that we could watch it. The storm had subsided, and during the afternoon the sun shone out bright and warm and a high wind prevailed.

Sometime before night, a man and boy passed across the field not far from us, and the boy soon got his eyes on our canoe and cried out, "There's a canoe, pap!" They went down to it, and, from their actions, we saw that they were going to take it away. I spoke to Wood and told him that it would not do to allow them to do. so, and we walked out of the thicket on the further side from them, and leisurely came down to where they were, when I said:

"Hallo, there! what are you doing with that boat?

"I thought it had drifted here, and I was going to take care of it," was the reply.

"That is a government boat," said I. "We tied it up here awhile ago on account of the high wind."

I then repeated the boat story which we had before told at our last stopping-place This seemed to be an entirely satisfactory explanation to him.

I then said to Mark, "Do you think the wind will admit of our proceeding on our way to Chattanooga?"

The man spoke up, before Mark could answer, and said, "Men, I would not advise you to venture on the river now. It is not safe. You had better go down to the house, and wait till the wind falls."

This proposition suited us well enough, under the circumstances, so we accepted his invitation, and accompanied him to his cabin. We found his wife a very talkative old lady. She sympathized heart and soul, she said, with soldiers, for she had a son in the army, who sent word home that he had a pretty hard time of it.

Night came, but the wind still blew a gale. They invited us to stay all night with them, but we told them that it was absolutely necessary that we should be back to camp by the next day, if possible. We had learned, in the meantime, that we were only five miles above Chattanooga, and we timed our start so as to pass there at the most favorable time.

CHAPTER VI.

Running by Chattanooga—A Dangerous Voyage—Through Whirlpools and Rapids—Lucky Encounter With a Log—Taking On a Pilot—A Terrific Ride—Hailed By Rebel Cavalry—Reconnoitering a Rebel Camp at Bridgeport—A Rebel Stampede—Arrival at Stevenson—Fatal Mistake—Cause of the Stampede—Captured Within Seven Miles of Mitchell's Lines—A Story that Didn't Win—Sent to Bridgeport Under Guard—"These Are the Two Train-Thieves We Have Been Looking After so Long."

ABOUT midnight the wind went down, and we pushed out in our little boat and long before daylight we were quietly drifting past Chattanooga, that most "ticklish" point. When we had fairly passed that dreaded city, we felt that the greatest part of our task was over. We began to imagine ourselves almost back again among our old comrades of the Twenty-First. We felt encouraged and jubilant. We soon found, however, that it was not to be all smooth sailing yet.

Some ten or fifteen miles below the city, the river runs through a deep gorge, and narrows down to only a small proportion of its former width. The mountains rise abruptly from the water in frowning grandeur, while great rocks, from dizzy heights, project out over the rushing, foaming torrent below. To increase the troubles of navigation here, the river makes a sharp turn to the left, after a long, straight stretch, during which time the water gathers great velocity of motion, and suddenly dashes against the wall of rock at the elbow, recoils, and forms a great, rapid, foaming eddy, after which it rushes on down the gorge in mad fury, as if trying to get revenge for the check it has just received. We perceived, even in the darkness, that there was danger ahead. The great roar and noise caused by the dashing of the angry waters against the rocks warned us. We hugged the left bank with our little boat as closely as possible. As we passed the angry whirlpool, into which we seemed to be drifting, our boat was struck a tremendous blow by a floating log. We thought we were all dashed to pieces. The blow hoisted us away, however, several yards to the left, and we went flying down the gorge like the wind. We were afterwards told that a number of adventurous persons had, at different times, lost their lives in trying to run down this place, by getting swamped in this great torrent, or whirlpool, and it was, no doubt, owing to the blow received by the floating log, by which our boat was knocked just beyond the reach of danger, that we escaped as fortunately as we did. It was a providential blow for us, although it came well nigh crushing our boat. We pulled at our paddles with might and main to keep the water from swamping our boat, which sank pretty low in the current and was now going at railroad speed. We soon reached smoother water, and again felt ourselves safe.

It was now getting light, and, as we drifted on, we saw a man on shore motioning with all his might for us to approach him. As there seemed to be something unusual about his actions, we pulled in a little, when he hailed us and said if we went on as we were then going, we would be drowned in spite of fate. He said, "You are strangers in these parts, ain't you?" We told him we had never been down the river before although quite familiar with the country. He then said, "Strangers, whatever you do, don't try to run down through the 'suck.' I have lived here all my life, and have known men who were well acquainted with the river, to be drowned there. It is much worse than the place you have just passed."

We tried to persuade him to go with us and pilot us down, but he said he was not well. At last, however, with much urging and the promise of three dollars, he consented to go. We rowed to the shore, and, after providing himself with an extra paddle, he came aboard and took charge of our craft, which we ran as close to the left shore as possible. The water ran with such great velocity and force that we found it almost impossible to control the boat, although we all had paddles, and were pulling as if for life. Our new pilot understood his business well and knew how to man a boat.

At the place where we apprehended most danger, the river runs through a narrow gorge. The whole volume of water, thus circumscribed, draws right to the center of the channel. After a ride which I never wish to repeat, we passed in safety, with no further mishap than getting our boat nearly full of water, which we soon bailed out. Our pilot now gave us careful directions as to the course we should take in the river below, after which we dismissed him, first paying him three dollars, which we felt had been a good investment, as we would have doubtless been drowned, but for the accidental fact of meeting this man. Though it had been our practice to travel only in the night, yet we had been compelled, through the difficulty of navigating this part of the river, to travel in daylight, which was imprudent, as we were constantly reminded.

I may state just here a fact, which is well known to all men, who, in time of war, have tried to escape from prison. The most critical part of a journey is that which lies immediately between the two contending armies. At such places, between the two hostile lines, patrols are constantly moving about. Outposts are established on all important roads, while vidette and picket posts, in command of the most active and vigilant officers, are constantly on the alert for spies, scouts, or prowling bands of cavalrymen from the enemy's camp. Every stray man is picked up and sent to the officer of the guard, who either sends him to the guard-house, or to the General at headquarters, and if the unfortunate fellow does not tell a pretty straight story, or if there is anything suspicious about his appearance, he is put under strict guard, and, perhaps, ordered tried by a drumhead court martial, charged with being a spy. It is the worst place in the world to be caught fooling around —this ground between two hostile armies in camp. A man is almost certain to be captured, unless he is well posted, and, if captured, he must give a very strict account of himself.

As before stated, we found it unsafe to travel in daytime, and, shortly after dismissing our pilot, we spied a squad of rebel cavalry on the right bank of the river.

Luckily, the river was pretty wide at that place, and we chanced to be well to the far side from them. They yelled to us to come ashore, but we pretended not to hear them, and acted as if we were intending to land leisurely on the far side, We were too far away for convenient musket range, and did not fear them much, but the circumstance caused us to think it best to land a few miles below, and secrete both ourselves and the boat.

During the voyage of the following night, or rather just before daylight, we passed the Bridgeport railroad crossing. We could see the guards on the bridge, but did not know whether they were rebels or Yankees, so in this uncertainty we let our boat drift quietly with the current, and passed by unnoticed. We supposed confidently that General Mitchell had occupied Bridgeport. So after we had passed below the bridge, out of sight, we landed, and Mark remained with the boat while I stole up to the camp to find out what kind of soldiers were there. It did not take me long, however, to discover that they wore butternut uniforms, and I hurried back to the canoe. Mark's disappointment knew no bounds. I could scarcely convince him that I told the truth.

About sunrise we stopped and hid our canoe, and feeling somewhat hungry, and also anxious to learn something about the Federals, we concluded to skulk off a short distance, and see what we could find. It was not long until we found a cabin, where we got breakfast and learned that the Yankees were at Stevenson, or a short distance the other side. Soon after leaving this cabin we met a squad of soldiers in full retreat. They told us that we had better be "lighting out;" that the roads and woods were "alive with the d—d Yankee cavalry. They are in Stevenson and pushing on this way in heavy force." We expressed some little apprehension, but went on a little further, when we met more rebel militia, who told us the same story. It seemed as if there was a regular stampede among them.

We now became pretty well convinced that if we could get safely to Stevenson we would be all right. So we went back to our canoe and rowed down the river again, until we thought we were about opposite the town, which is about four miles north from the river. Then we tied up the canoe and struck out through the woods for the town. Just before reaching the place, we had to cross a creek, after which we ascended a very long, steep hill. When we had reached the top of this hill, we were somewhat surprised to find ourselves right in the town, but not half so much astonished as we were to find no blue-coats there, but the streets swarming with rebel soldiers. We had been wofully deceived by the stories of the frightened fugitives we had met in the forenoon, and had unwarily entrapped ourselves.

Wood proposed that we should start and run, but I saw that course would not answer, so we determined to put on a bold front, and take our chances, though we knew we ran great risk. We met and spoke with a number of soldiers. Some of the officers noticed us carelessly, while others paid no attention to us as we passed them. We went into a store and bought some tobacco, and inquired for some other trifling things, and then started off as unconcernedly as if we were a couple of country fellows, accustomed to visiting the town. We had gone some little distance, when we were met by an officer, who stopped us, and said that he would have to inquire our business there, and who we were. These were pointed questions, but we knew it would be necessary to meet them. We told him who we were and all about it, and he appeared well satisfied with our answers and was about to dismiss us, when, unfortunately for us, another man, I think a citizen, came up, and, pointing at me, said:

"That is one of the d—d rascals that was here last night. He rode through the town, cutting all the flourishes he knew how. I know him. He dare not deny it, either."

In explanation of this man's singular, unexpected, and to us fatal accusation, I will say that I afterwards learned that a squad of daring troopers, from the Fourth Ohio Cavalry, had, on the previous night, made a reckless dash into the place, cutting and slashing on all sides, stampeding the whole town, and running out the few rebel cavalry stationed there, who supposed that General Mitchell's whole column was upon them. After doing this the troopers galloped out again, and left the bewildered rebels as much surprised because of their leaving, as they had by their unexpected coming. This also explains the stories told us by the flying fugitives, who had, by their silly fright, beguiled us into the rebel camp.

As soon as we were thus detained, I directed all my attention to destroying the map in my possession, by tearing it in pieces in my pocket, dropping portions of it, whenever opportunity offered, and chewing up much of it, until I finally succeeded, without detection, in disposing of the whole of it. Had this map been discovered in my possession, it would have been strong evidence against us, and it was, therefore, a great relief, when the last vestige of it had disappeared.

This man's story ended all hope of our getting away, and we were prisoners a second time. No sooner was attention once directed to us than we were surrounded, and scores of fellows saw in our appearance something suspicious. We told the most plausible story we could invent, but it was of no use. They now searched us, and found our revolvers, which was evidence against us, but, fortunately, found nothing more calculated to reveal our true characters. It made but little difference, however, in the end, for they were in a high state of excitement at that time, and in spite of our protestations of innocence, we were bundled off under guard, put on a hand-car and run up to Bridgeport, where the commanding officer was stationed.

We reached Bridgeport soon after dark, and there we were again stripped and searched. Boots, hats, coats, socks and every under-garment underwent the strictest scrutiny. They could find nothing, and were about on a stand as to what judgment to pass on our cases, when fate again turned against us by interposing a circumstance which ended all hope in our favor. An excited fellow, who came and stuck his head in among the gaping crowd, who were staring at us, declared, in a loud voice, that we belonged to Andrews' spies and train-thieves.

All eyes were turned on him instantly, my own

among them. Of course, he felt bound to back up the assertion, although I believe he lied, at least such were my feelings. The spirit of resentment rose up within me, until I could have killed him without compunction, if I had possessed the power, for in the next breath he said, “I know those fellows! I saw them on the train!”

The commanding officer stared at us with a look of exultant surprise, and said, “I’ll bet any money, by G—d, that these are the two men we have been looking after so long. These are two of the villains that have not been captured.”

CHAPTER VII.

Strongly Guarded—General Leadbetter at Bridgeport—Red Hot Interview with the Scoundrel—A Blustering Braggart and an Arrant Coward—Separate Examination of Wood and Myself—Taken back to Chattanooga—Parting Words with Leadbetter—"The Hole" —Dungeon and Chains—Old Swims, the Jailer—A Horrible, Loathsome Pit, Crowded with Miserable, Helpless Human Beings—Loaded with Chains.

> "Oh! how I wished for spear or sword,
> At least to die amidst the horde,
> And perish—if it must be so—
> At bay, destroying many a foe."

WE were at once taken to the guard-house, and a strong guard, with loaded muskets and fixed bayonets, encircled us during the entire night, at least fifty soldiers performing that duty. With their noise, we could get but little sleep, and escape was wholly out of the question, although we kept a vigilant watch for such an opportunity.

In all probability they had telegraphed to General Leadbetter, that night, who was at Chattanooga, for he was at Bridgeport the next morning, and our first acquaintance with that official took place while we were cooking our rations, some raw pork, at a fire, near the guard-house. While thus engaged, he came up to us, and seemed anxious to gratify a fiendish sort of curiosity, and satisfy himself, on actual view, that we were the right men. He took off our hats and carefully examined our complexions. He at once pronounced us Yankees. He said we had been accustomed to wearing the little, round regulation caps in the Federal army. Said he, "These fellows are a d—d good prize. The last one of them shall be hung, too."

He told us that Andrews, the leader of the gang, was to be hung that day, and, probably, would get his just deserts before we reached Chattanooga. He talked in this threatening, brow-beating style, no doubt, with the expectation of intimidating or scaring us into making some admissions that could be used as evidence. When he found that this sort of bombast made no impression on us, he changed tacties a little, and, after quite a pause, said, "Well, boys, whether you are the men or not, it was a d—d bold stroke. I suppose old Mitchell picked and culled over the whole Yankee army to find the most reckless, hardened men he could." Then he again said. "I'll be d—d if I don't hang the last one of you."

I said to him, "Hang and be d—d; but I will tell you one thing to remember. If you ever do come across one of Mitchell's men, and hang him, look out that sooner or later your own neck don't pay the penalty; because," I continued, "this hanging business will be quite common about the time the rebellion closes up."

He looked as though he had half a mind to cut me down with his sword, on the spot, but said not a word. He soon after walked away, and we could hear him giving directions to the officer of the guard to observe the greatest caution, "for," said he, "those fellows are hard customers, and will take advantage of the least opportunity offered to break away. They are afraid of nothing, nor will they hesitate to run any risk, no matter how great." The officer told him that we would not get away alive, as he had an eye on us all the time.

We ate our rations without further molestation, after which we were again placed in the guard-house, and it was not long until my companion, Mark Wood, was taken out and put through a long, searching ordeal of cross-questioning, until he perspired like a man in a July harvest. The examination was conducted in an open space in front of the guard-house and surrounded by hundreds of soldiers and eager listeners. What Wood told them, or how well he made his story appear, I do not know, but without doubt the poor fellow was entrapped and confused.

My thoughts and feelings during the time while I was awaiting my turn to undergo their thorough cross-questioning, can better be imagined than described. I saw plainly that we were fairly in their clutches—that there was no use of hoping further. After all our hardships, and after getting back to within seven miles of General Mitchell's picket-posts, to be picked up and confronted with these spy charges, supported by some damning circumstances against us—enough at least to lead to our final detection—was enough to drive any one to thoughts of desperation.

As Wood came in he whispered to me and said, "No use to deny it; they've found out by some means." I was at once ordered out, and now confronted by General Leadbetter, some idea of whose character may be gleaned from Parson Brownlow's Book. He was nothing more nor less than a contemptible drunken bully, a profane, blustering braggart, and withal a most arrant coward.

He asked me if I knew anything about Andrews or the party that had been with him. I had determined to admit nothing—to deny everything, and to avoid saying anything which might possibly conflict with what Wood might have said—in fact, I meant to say but little. When, therefore, I denied any knowledge of Andrews' party, he looked at me as though he would look clear through me, then burst out in a towering passion, and said:

"Will you stand up here and tell such a d—d lie as that? you infernal scoundrel—you abominable Yankee vagabond! Now speak the truth, sir!"

I had been looking him straight in the eye from the moment he began speaking to me. I now felt that degree of reckless desperation that I had never felt before, which was intensified by his stinging insult and overbearing manner. He had addressed me as if I had been a slave or a cowardly menial. Though I was perfectly self-controlled, I felt the hot blood coursing to my brain, and my hair seemed to be rising on end. I was in a frame of mind to do anything. Thoughts of murder flashed through my brain. I took my eyes from the old rebel villain for an instant, and cast a hasty glance around for a club or something, with which I intended instantly to brain him. I called on his men to throw me a club—anything, with which I could teach their "d—d, sand-lapping, son-of-a-b—brigadier, how to speak to a gentleman, and, also to give him a chance to practice sword-exercise at the same time." No more opprobrious epithet, or one of greater indignity can be applied to a person in the South than that of "sand-lapper." I did not deign to speak to *him*, but addressed his men, and I heaped every opprobrious epithet on his head that I could think of. He was an overbearing, mean officer, and I believe his men would have rejoiced, and willingly have helped me to something to have ended his miserable life if they had dared to do so. He saw that I was bent on mischief, for he kept his eyes on me some moments, and then spoke out and said:

"Men, don't you take your eyes off of that man or he will go through the whole d—d mess of you. He's a hard case."

The next time he spoke to me he had changed his tone very much, and addressed me as one man ordinarily should another. He took a paper from his pocket and read our names, "John A. Wilson and Mark Wood," and asked me if I knew either of them. I said I did not.

He pretended to be astonished, and said, "It is a strange thing that you do not know them. I will tell you who they are. Mark Wood is in the guard-tent yonder, and John A. Wilson is standing before me. You need not deny it any more. We have men who saw you on the train, and would know you any place. Your comrade has had to acknowledge it and so will you.

"Well," I said, "you can have it as you d—d please. I am a prisoner, and you have the power, and I see you have also the disposition, to convict me, whether innocent or guilty."

I was sent back to the guard-tent; but we did not stay there long. The train that was to take us to Chattanooga soon arrived, to which we were conducted under a strong guard, and were soon on our way back to Chattanooga. The very thought of that place oppressed me. I dreaded to go back there. I knew it meant evil to us. I could have willingly jumped from the train, even had I known that my life would have been sacrificed; but on we sped, our thoughts filled with the most gloomy apprehensions for the future.

It was not long after we started, that General Leadbetter came into the car in which Wood and I were seated. His bearing was much modified toward us. In a very gentlemanly manner he requested Wood, who was in the same seat with me, to take another seat, as he wished to have a rational talk with me, if I had no objection. I replied that I was perfectly willing to talk with him, and that the manner of the conversation would depend much on himself. He took the seat Wood had vacated, and began talking very pleasantly. We had quite a long conversation in regard to various matters.

During the conversation I noticed that he was adroitly trying to lead me into admissions that would have been inconsistent with my former statements, or that would have been damaging evidence against us. But I carefully avoided being led into any such admissions, or in making any statement that would betray our true characters.

When the train arrived at Chattanooga, he arose and shook hands with us, and regretted our unfortunate situation—"for," said he, "whatever may be your crime, you are brave men, and you engaged in a job that but few men would care to attempt. Had you been a day sooner, you would have succeeded."

I perceived the drift of this, and told him in substance, that if we had been of the raiding party, we might possibly feel complimented by his remarks, and that I hoped his sympathy for our unfortunate situation would go so far as to cause him to see that we had a fair trial, and were not convicted if innocent.

In a few moments we were marched to prison, surrounded by armed guards, and here our sorrows and hardships began in earnest. The guard conducted us to a room, where we were handcuffed and chained together with a large chain each end of which was fastened about our necks. We were then conducted to another room, in the center of which was a trap-door, fastened down with bolts and locks. An old white-haired man, with a hard, withered-looking face, and a treble-sounding voice, was jailer. He was a hardened old wretch, who loved whisky and despised "Yankees," as he called all Northern people. His name was Swims. He moved about in a bustling, shuffling gait, as though he were making a great effort to be in a hurry. He drew from his pocket a large key, and getting down on his knees, applied it to the great rusty locks on the trap-door. The fastenings were soon released, and with great effort he lifted the heavy door on its hinges, while an attendant brought a long ladder, which was run down the hole, and we were ordered to descend.

As we stepped forward to obey the command, I caught a breath of the horrible stench and foul, hot air, which came up through that revolting hole. I involuntarily stepped back. I never had smelled so loathsome and sickening a stench before, and despairingly looked around to see if there was no other alternative. The threatening bayonets of the guard reminded us that there was no choice left. We sullenly crawled down as well as our chain would admit. Down, down we went into that suffocating, dark dungeon. Sepulchral voices and specter-like forms admonished us that others had gone down before us, but it was not until we had reached the foot of the ladder that we found that the stinking, loathsome pit was crowded with miserable human beings, smothering and gasping for breath.

It was with difficulty we could get a place to stand. As soon as we were off the ladder it was taken up and the trap-door shut down, when it was so dark that we could not see anything. After considerable crowding and squeezing, we found standing room. We could not see to tell who or what our companions in misery were, but soon heard familiar voices, and we had said but a word or so, when some one spoke out and said:

"My God, that is Wilson and Wood! Good Heavens! they have got every one of us!"

The poor fellows crowded around us, and such a babel and confusion of talk it would be hard to describe. The party had all been captured for some time, except ourselves, and they had believed and hoped that we had made good our escape. They told us that Andrews, our leader, was then on trial for his life, and that there was no doubt of his conviction and execution, while the prospect for the rest of us was not a whit better. They all seemed resigned to their fate, and were even anx-

GOING DOWN INTO DARKNESS.

ious for the day to come and relieve them from the torments of this vile dungeon. Death, they said, would be a welcome relief.

This den was thirteen feet square and thirteen feet deep. There were two small holes in the sides, one of which had been nearly choked up by the earth caving in against it, and both were so obstructed by iron bars that but little air could get through—barely enough to keep the wretched inmates from smothering to death.

CHAPTER VIII.

Horror upon Horrors—Torture and Torment well-nigh Unendurable—Loathsome Corn-bread and Rotten Meat—Odors Most Foul
—Fetters, Vermin and Darkness—Parallel with the Black Hole of Calcutta—A Very Hell on Earth—The Boom of Mitchell's Cannon—A Night of Anxiety—Sad Disappointment—Off to Atlanta—A Soldier's Life—A Bloodthirsty Mob Clamoring for our Lives—Landed in Better Quarters at Madison—Visited by a Union Spy—The Spy's Narrow Escape—Back to our Chattanooga Prison—The Heroic Lad, Jacob Parrott, Brutally Whipped on the Naked Back.

"As I lay on the damp, cold ground,
I felt a shudder o'er me creep,
To know that I was weak, and bound
captive there. I knew not why
The blood was frozen in my veins;
Thou know'st I do not fear to die,
And yet I trembled in my chains."

IN this loathsome dungeon every man of our entire party, twenty-two in all, was incarcerated, including Porter and Hawkins, who, it will be remembered, were left at Marietta on the morning of the raid. They also had been subsequently captured, and here we were all together. Besides our party, there were also twelve or fifteen other prisoners, most of them East Tennessee Union men, and one negro, who had been in there seven months and had five months more to stay. The charge against him, as I understood at the time, was that of trying to escape from bondage, and, when arrested, refusing to tell where he belonged. He was taken out occasionally and mercilessly whipped and beaten to force him to divulge. We felt much sympathy for the poor, friendless creature, who was known by the name of Aleck, for he not only bore his torments without complaint, but tried in every way to comfort and encourage his fellow prisoners in their distress. He ministered to our wants cheerfully, in every way that lay in his power, and proved himself an invaluable friend and assistant. When the time of his sentence should expire, he was to be put up at auction and sold into bondage again.

To aggravate our torments and make our lives more intolerable, we were being literally eaten up by vermin—lice. There were both bed-bugs and fleas, but they were as nothing compared with the lice which swarmed over our bodies, night and day, by millions. We were hand-cuffed and chained in pairs, so that it was impossible to strip off our clothing and temporarily rid ourselves of them, even if there had been sufficient light to have done so. We could scrape up a handful of sand from the floor, and carry it to the sickly ray of light shed in between the bars at the window, and it would be alive with lice.

I have heard of the *"Black Hole" of Calcutta,

*The Black Hole, a military dungeon in Fort William, Calcutta, India, is noted for being the scene of one of the most tragical events in English history. Mr. Holwell, one of the survivors of the horrible affair, gives the following account of it: "On the capture of Calcutta by Surajah Dowlah, June 20, 1756, the British garrison, consisting of one hundred and forty-six men, under the command of Mr. Holwell, were taken prisoners and locked up for the night in the common dungeon of the fortress, a strongly-barred room, eighteen feet square, and never intended for the confinement of more than two or three men at a time. There were only two windows, both opening toward the west, whence, under the best of circumstances, but little air could enter. A few moments sufficed to throw them into profuse where the semi-barbarians of India suffocated a band of English prisoners to death, but I cannot believe their sufferings much surpassed the hellish torments inflicted upon us by these chivalrous, high-toned aristocrats of Southern-civilization. If old Leadbetter is alive yet, he deserves the fate of Wirz. If he is dead, and there is a hell and endless torture, there is little necessity for such an abode if he has escaped the torments of the damned. He was a heartless, inhuman devil, callous to all instincts of humanity, deaf to the appeals of brave men gasping and begging for that which God made free to all—the breath of life.

Many of the men had raw sores on them, caused by these myriads of vermin. We had no blankets to sleep on, and most of the men had become ragged and nearly naked in their night wanderings through the brush in

---

perspiration, the natural consequence of which was a raging thirst. They stripped off their clothes to gain more room, sat down on the floor that the air might circulate more freely, and, when every expedient failed, sought by the bitterest insults to provoke the guards to fire on them. One of the soldiers stationed in the verandah, was offered one thousand rupees to have them removed to a larger room. He went away, but returned saying it was impossible. The bribe was then doubled, and he made a second attempt with like result; the nabob was asleep and no one durst wake him. By 9 o'clock several had died, and many more were delirious. A frantic cry for water now became general, and one of the guards, more compassionate than his fellows, caused some to be brought to the bars, where Mr. Holwell and two or three others received it, in their hats, and passed it on to the men behind. In their impatience to secure it nearly all was spilt, and the little they drank seemed only to increase their thirst. Self-control was soon lost, those in remote parts of the room struggled to reach the window, and a fearful tumult ensued, in which the weakest were trampled or pressed to death. They raved, fought, prayed, blasphemed, and many then fell exhausted on the floor, where suffocation put an end to their torments. The Indian soldiers, meanwhile, crowded around the windows, and even brought lights that they might entertain themselves with the dreadful spectacle. The odor which filled the dungeon became more deadly every moment, and about 11 o'clock the prisoners began to drop off fast. At length, at 6 o'clock in the morning, Surajah Dowlah awoke, and ordered the door to be opened. Of the one hundred and forty-six, only twenty-three remained alive, and they were either stupefied or raving."

trying to escape. However, we had but little need of clothing in this suffocating dungeon, as the weather was getting very hot, and this, with the difficulty of free breathing, kept us almost in a constant state of perspiration. The fetid air and the stifling heat also caused us to be tormented with great thirst. We could not all find sleeping room at one time—that is, to lie down and sleep. When the cool part of the night came, and we were overcome with weariness, some would recline against the walls, while others would sit up and lean against their comrade next to them, and still others, more fortunate than the rest, would find a spot large enough to curl up and lie down, only to be trodden on, perhaps, by some poor fellows groping about in the dark for water to quench their thirst. Sometimes these unintentional accidents would cause sharp contentions in the night, for our miserable condition did not render our tempers the sweetest in the world.

My wrists had become so swollen above and below the iron bands that the iron had sunk into the flesh almost out of sight. In this painful condition, I had a comrade take my handkerchief and tie my elbows as closely together as possible, and day after day would I rest my bound arms, first over one shoulder and then over the other. This relieved the pain and swelling some, although it made me almost helpless, and it did seem as though the lice would devour me alive, swarming, as they did, over every portion of my body. Our condition was most pitiable—it was simply horrible.

But it was useless to complain. Our sufferings were

regarded by the officers with unfeeling, heartless indifference, even to insult. My defiant language to Leadbetter and the Bridgeport officers had, I suppose, made me the object of the special hatred of Leadbetter, who, I think, purposely put this needless infliction on me by instruction to the officer in charge.

Each morning, about nine o'clock usually, old Swims, the jailer, would raise the trap and call out, "men, here's your feed," which he lowered to us in a bucket attached to a rope. In the same manner our scanty supply of water was lowered to us. Our "feed" was a meager supply of corn-bread and half-rotten boiled bacon. This was given us twice a day, It required a pretty good stomach and appetite to swallow it, for not unfrequently we would find dead maggots in the stinking, unsavory mess. We were generally hungry enough, however, to eat anything we could get, good or bad. In the matter of rations, I suppose we fared no worse than Federal prisoners at Andersonville and other places, perhaps not as bad, yet we found it barely sufficient to sustain life.

Some of our party had some Confederate money left, and occasionally, as long as it lasted, they would hire old Swims to buy bread for us. The old rascal would sometimes take the money, and, after waiting a day or so, and hearing nothing of it, we would ask him about it, when he would tell us he had *lost it.* The probable truth was that he had used it to buy a few drams with. But we were at his mercy, and had to treat him with great civility and take his statements for facts, whether we believed them or not. No person, who has not been a prisoner, can form any correct conception of our utter degradation and suffering, while shut up in this vile place.

Curious visitors, who came to look down the trap-hole at us, spared no pains to show their contempt for "Old Abe's abolition dogs," as they called us. They regarded us as a crowd of reckless desperadoes, sent out on a mission of destruction and carnage. Occasionally some wordy disputes and arguments would spring up, for some of our crowd were pretty "tonguey," and generally gave as good as they received, and could call as hard names as their rebel visitors could. Seldom was the trap opened that there were not curious visitors, who would peer down, and generally they had something to say to us. We remained in this place of torment several weeks after Wood and I arrived; I do not know exactly how long, but it did seem to us, from all indications, that we were to be kept there until death relieved us.

At length, one afternoon, there was a great commotion and running to and fro, and galloping of horses outside, and very soon the trap was opened and the ladder thrust down, when we were ordered to crawl out, which command, it is needless to say, we obeyed as hurriedly as our helpless condition would allow. We were headed for the depot, where, several weeks before, we had voluntarily assembled, a free, hopeful and unfettered band, to take a ride on that same railroad.

Some of the poor fellows were so weak, and had been so long deprived of the free use of their limbs, that they could scarcely walk. We were all so blinded by the light that it was comical to see our bedazed, staggering efforts to walk. We must have appeared like a crowd of tipsy men, which furnished sport for the rebel guards, and gave them an excuse to abuse us roundly and threaten us with their bayonets. After we had been out awhile, our eyes became partially accustomed to the strong light, and we got along better.

We now learned what was "up." The Federal forces had appeared on the hills across the river, opposite the town and already the boom of Mitchell's cannon could be heard reverberating down the river and among the hills. All was confusion and chaos. The conductor on the train on which we were to go, had evidently taken fright; at any rate, he had pulled out ahead of time, and was already beyond the reach of Mitchell's guns. We were only too glad that the train had left, though we made no outward show of our feelings. We hoped that General Mitchell would push across the river and capture the town and thus release us.

We were returned to the dungeon for the night. That was a night of the greatest anxiety to us, as it was to the rebels of the city. Mitchell could easily have captured the place, had he only known its weakness. The rebels had but a small force, and were prepared to leave on short notice. We could hear the Federal shells bursting promiscuously about, and we were certain, that early next morning we should hear the Federal skirmish line at work in the suburbs of the town. What joyful music that would have been to our ears.

But, alas, our great expectations were disappointed. The morning came, but no clash of arms or sound of battle greeted our ears. Bright and early we were again taken to the depot, and this time the train was there. We vainly cast wishful eyes in the direction of the far bank of the river, but no rescuing friends were in sight, and our hopes sunk as low as our expectations had been high on the previous night.

Such is the life of a soldier—ever subject to the caprices of fickle fortune—to-day rejoicing, to-morrow sorrowing—to-day feasting, to-morrow starving—to-day shouting pæans of victory with his rejoicing comrades—to-morrow on the gallows, in the prison, or filling a soldier’s grave. And such is the rapidity with which these extremes of fortune follow in time of war, that one almost grows bewildered in his anxiety to keep pace with them.

As the train rolled on, we soon came to the scene of our former fearful ride. I could look from the cars and see the same brush where Mark and I so successfully secreted ourselves, and when I thought of the long, hard, fruitless struggle we had to escape, and how nearly we had reached our friends and safety, and then realized our present condition—in misery and chains, like felons, with the gallows’ doom pending over us, my heart and hope almost sunk within me.

But man is a singular compound after all. No despair is so black but that hope will quickly alternate, if we allow the mind free scope. A merciful God has so created us. He has implanted large hope in the human breast. Man hopes, in this uncertain life, to the last, and when bereft of all hope with which he clings to this world, he still hopes for a blessed Immortality beyond. I have seen this forcibly illustrated with one of my beloved comrades—a professed disbeliever, yet a brave man—standing on the brink of the dark shore of eternity, and of whom I shall speak hereafter in my narrative. Poor fellow! though he had often denied it, when his last hour had come—when all worldly hope was gone—he, too, had hope of Immortality.

As we went whirling past bridges and parts of the road where we had, over a month before, wrought so much mischief, many were the quiet, jocular remarks made by some of our party. It seemed to have been known in advance, that the Yankee train-thieves and spies were going through to Atlanta. At any rate, at nearly every town there would be a crowd assembled to peer in on us through the windows. Northern people can scarcely believe how much curiosity the Southern people had to see a Yankee, more especially a Yankee soldier. The old soldiers will all remember this well. Some of the Southerners actually seemed to feel a superstitious belief about the Yankees. They imagined them to be some dreadful ogres or incarnate devils, who would steal a "nigger" as quick as a hawk would a chicken—who would burn houses, ravish women and steal gold watches, but wouldn't fight.

The fact of our coming into their midst and stealing a train had rather enhanced this belief, and we were, from appearances, regarded by these people as the very incarnation of Yankee vandalism. Soldiers, citizens and women, all, seemed possessed of this itching curiosity to see a veritable Yankee; but I have no doubt that many of them saw more Yankees than they cared to before the end of the Rebellion. What appeared to me cowardly and out of place on the part of soldiers and men in citizen's dress, was their habit of plying us with insulting epithets and tauntingly reminding us that our necks were sure of the halter. We answered them, not surer than theirs—that General Mitchell had a bad crowd with him, and that they would get heartily sick of rope performances before the game was ended.

Groups of ladies would come to the windows and gaze at us with absolute trembling, as if we were ferocious wild beasts. Some of these would express compassion for our having to be loaded with heavy chains while there was a strong military guard over us at the same time. We could overhear some of them talking. One would say "Why, some of them are smart, civil-looking fellows. It is a shame to treat them so. What if old Mitchell should get some of *our* men?" As a general thing, most of our crowd said but little, except when asked civil questions, which we as civilly answered. At Big Shanty, where we stole the train, there was a big crowd—more soldiers than citizens. They were pretty fierce, and would have done us violence but for the guards.

Our destination seemed to be Atlanta, or some place beyond, where jail room and a place of safety could be found. When we arrived at Atlanta the train stopped for some time, and the longer we were there the larger the crowd became. They swarmed in hundreds about the car we were in, to get a glimpse of us. This, it will be remembered, was in 1862, and before Sherman and his bummers had made the citizens of Atlanta so familiar with the appearance of Federal soldiers. The company of rebel guards, who had us in charge, were deployed about the car to keep the crowd back as much as possible. Part of the great throng exhibited a disposition to mob the prisoners, and were loud and demonstrative in their threats. The poor, cowardly sand-lappers and clay-eaters finally got so violent and uncontrollable, that the city provost-guards had to be brought to the assistance of the train-guards, to keep the howling mob from taking us from the cars and hanging us to the lamp posts. Their insulting screeches and clamor for vengeance could be heard from all sides. How I should like to have seen the old Twenty-First Regiment, under the command of the intrepid Colonel Arnold McMahan, turned loose by companies on that blood-thirsty, cowardly mob, who would insult and do violence to a few half-starved men loaded down with chains and shackles. This crudely-told incident is not a very strong support to the theory of the chivalrous valor and honor once so vauntingly claimed by the slaveholding aristocracy of the South.

I was very much relieved when the whistle sounded, and the train pulled out for Madison, Georgia, for I have no doubt that had we been detained fifteen minutes longer, we would have been dragged from the cars and hung, or cut to pieces, or beaten to death in the streets, so crazy and excited had these infuriated demons become. I was glad to leave them—that I am certain of.

Next morning we reached Madison, which was a neat, prettily-situated town, although the effects of war were visible in the deserted appearance of the streets, where no men were to be seen, except a few soldiers on leave of absence, or cripples, and occasionally an old man. On our march to the jail, groups of women and children thronged the sidewalks to stare at us.

We found the jail here a paradise, compared with our late den at Chattanooga. We had plenty of room, light, and. best of all, we had plenty of fresh air to breathe, and a fair supply of very tolerable rations. We would have been more comfortable if our chains and irons had been taken off, but, as it was, we recruited rapidly, and soon felt like men again, all of which blessings we appreciated, and were as devoutly thankful for as ever mortal men could be.

While we were here, many visitors came to see us. Among these, one day, an intelligent man came in, dressed in a neat Confederate uniform, and whom I noticed speaking hurriedly in a low tone of voice to Andrews. We did not suspect anything at the time, and from the decidedly rebel views he expressed to us, we took the officer for a rabid secesh, but after he had been gone some little time, Andrews privately communicated to us the fact that he was acquainted with the man, and the additional fact, surprising to us, that he was none other than a Federal spy, in the service of the United States. We trembled at the audacious daring of the fellow, and were wondering whether it could be possible that he was in fact, as Andrews said, a Union man running his neck into the very halter. We were inclined to doubt the correctness of the story, until a little later, the sergeant of the guard, who came in to bring our supper, told us that a remarkable thing had happened that afternoon.

The sergeant said the commandant of the town had learned, by some means, that one of Lincoln's spies had been among the visitors at the prison during the afternoon, and had at once put officers on the hunt for him to cause his arrest. The spy was found at the depot, just as the cars were coming' in. He became very indignant because of his arrest and told them, with great emphasis, that he had papers in his pocket that would prove his character anywhere. The officer of the guard was taken aback somewhat at this information, and released his hold on the stranger, but asked him to produce the papers. The spy thereupon thrust his hand in his pocket and began fumbling about, as though trying to find them. By this time the train had started, and the hind coach was just passing where they stood at a pretty good rate of speed, when he sprang from the guard like a tiger and got aboard the train. There was no telegraph office at the station and he made good his escape.

This caused the rebel commandant to forbid any more visiting; but we felt consolation in the hope that the spy would report our condition to the United States authorities and some efforts would be made to secure our release. Whether the spy ever reached the Union lines I do not know.

After a stay of several days at the Madison jail, an order came one day for our immediate return to Chattanooga, and the good time we were having was suddenly brought to a close. General Mitchell, though he had badly frightened the citizens and rebel soldiers, had not taken the town. We were hurried back and incarcerated in the same old prison we had been in before. Two circumstances, however, after our return, did much to relieve the misery of this prison The captain of the guard allowed a portion of our party to remain in the room above the pit, which was our first quarters.

This was a great relief, at least to some of us, and made more room for the others below. We had, also, with the assistance of a case-knife, which one of our men had secured, contrived implements by which we could unlock our shackles, and we were thus enabled to relieve ourselves of this discomfort, except at times when we expected the jailer in, when we would replace them, as otherwise, had they found out what was going on, they would have brought in a blacksmith and put them on to *stay*, besides cramming us all down into the "hole" again.

They must have regarded us as very desperate, dangerous men, from the extraordinary precautions they took. Even when we were all down in the hole, where there was no chance to escape, they would always bring a strong guard into the room before they would lift the trap-door, and now that we were in the upper room, a guard was kept on the outside of the fence around the prison, also one on the stairs which led to the second story, and when the jailer entered from his room in front of ours, a strong guard, with fixed bayonets, ready for instant use, was at his back. This extra precaution on their part only disclosed the fact that they had some serious reasons, serious to us at least, for guarding us so closely, and the further fact that they were afraid of us, even with our chains on, all of which did not in the least deter us, however, from laying plans to escape. To quiet us and as if to allay our apprehensions, and thus prevent any efforts on our part to regain our liberty, our guards talked encouragingly about our being exchanged like other prisoners.

Unfortunately, some of our men were beguiled by

this seductive talk, and by it, a premeditated effort to escape, which at least promised success, was thwarted. To those of us who looked the matter squarely in the face, there was, in the very nature of the rebels' course of treatment of our party, something that boded evil and forbade the thought or hope of an exchange, as in the case of ordinary prisoners of war. First, we were not sent into camp with other Union prisoners they held. Again, we discovered when we were all together and compared notes, that every means had been resorted to by our incensed captors to extort and obtain admissions and confessions from us, which could be used as evidence on which to support charges for our conviction. Of course, they must put us through the *form*, at least, of a trial and sustain their charges by some kind of testimony, by which our execution would have the appearance of justification under the rules of civilized warfare, otherwise the Federals would be justified before the world, in swift and terrible retaliation.

The rebels had shown an especial desire to find out who was the leader of our band, and also the engineer—the man who ran the locomotive to death in our great race. Those two men they seemed to regard as the head and front of the offense—the men whose lives were first to be sacrificed on the altar of rebel vengeance. But, I am proud to be able to say, that not a man of that faithful band was base enough to betray his comrades, although poor Jacob Parrott, of the Thirty-Third Ohio, the youngest of the party, and who had a boyish appearance, was stripped naked by the inhuman devils who captured him near Ringgold the same day we left the engine, and four men held him stretched hand and foot on a large rock, while others held revolvers to his head, threatening him with instant death if he made the least effort at resistance. Having thus placed him, a rebel lieutenant scored and gashed his naked back with a heavy raw-hide to make him confess, and more especially to tell the names of the leader and engineer. Thrice was he released and asked to confess, and thrice put to the torture because he refused, until his inhuman captors had sickened and tired of the inhuman spectacle before them, for, although they had whipped him until his back was one mass of bloody welts, and bruised, quivering, lacerated flesh, still did the heroic lad refuse to open his lips and disclose a word that might, betray his comrades. He suffered untold agonies from this merciless lashing. His back became a mass of sores, and with the hard floor to lie on, and no covering, it was no wonder that his affliction nearly cost him his life. This undaunted hero is living at Kenton, Ohio, and still carries the scars of that terrible deed.

CHAPTER IX.

Planning to Escape—Lured by False Hopes—Night Fixed upon for the Attempt—Twelve of the Train-Thieves Sent to Knoxville for Trial—Escape Postponed—Andrews' Death-Warrant —A Solemn Occasion—Preparations to Break Jail- Andrews, the Spy, and. John. Wollam Escape—The Guards Aroused—The Pursuit—Andrews' Wanderings and Terrible Sufferings —Three Days Almost Naked—Recaptured on an Island in the River—Bruised, Bleeding and Torn, He is Brought Back to the Prison More Dead than Alive.

"Fly, Fleance, fly! thou mayst escape."

THIS course of the rebel authorities towards our band had a significance—a meaning, which to me, and, in fact, to most of us, was not pleasant to think of. It forbade the thought—yea, the possibility—of our being exchanged. Andrews, our leader, with a noble magnanimity and the courage of a lion, had admitted to them that he was the leader of the party, and, as before noted, had been out and had a trial, or what purported to be such, before a court-martial, the findings and sentence of which had not yet been made known, and he had been returned to the prison with us to await the result.

Meantime we had carefully canvassed our chances of escape. There were two plans, and only two, in which the chances of success looked fairly reasonable, and even in these the odds were as five to one against us. Still, they offered a possibility, and, to men in our desperate situation, no risk was too great.

One of these plans was that we should all have our irons off in the evening when the jailer and guards came up to bring our supper, and as soon as the door was opened, make a grand rush on the leveled bayonets, disarm the guards, rush down on the guards below, and disarm them; then, taking the arms thus secured, we could have marched in a solid body to the ferry-boat, which lay on our side of the river, cross over, destroy the boat or disable her, and escape to the mountains, where no ordinary squad of mounted troopers could have captured us.

The other plan, proposed by Andrews, the most feasible, and the one finally agreed upon, was, that one of our number should, as we came in from our breathing spell in the yard—which, by order of Colonel Claiborne, Provost Marshal, we had been allowed part of the time since our return to this prison, and for which, and other acts of humanity, he was removed from his position by Leadbetter—conceal himself under the jailer's bed, in the room in front of us, and then, after everything was quiet at night, steal out, noiselessly unlock the door, after which we could all come out, go stealthily down stairs in a body, surprise and disarm the guard, and then proceed to the boat as in the other plan.

All were anxious, if I remember rightly, except two, Marion Ross and George D. Wilson, the latter of Cincinnati, who thought the proposed attempt premature. They relied on the talk of the officers in charge of us, that we would be exchanged—a reliance, based on a sandy foundation, as will be seen from a coincidence, which will be mentioned further along in my account, and which recalls the names of these two comrades. But there were some flying reports and rumors current that did, for a little time, cause a rainbow of hope to appear in our cheerless, cloudy horizon. These and the opposition, more especially of Wilson, who was a ready talker, well educated, full of experience, fertile and ingenious in resources, a close reasoner, and had much influence with us, temporarily lulled the clamor for bouncing the guards and trying to escape. Yet, although I was in the minority, I did not feel, nor do I now feel satisfied that the attempt was not both justifiable and feasible. I would not, however, be understood as reflecting on the judgment of any of my comrades, many of whom have gone beyond the reach of voice or sight of man. We were all trying to do for the best, though we differed in judgment. Yet, I have learned by experience that when a fellow is in a tight place, especially where his life and liberty are at stake, prompt, decisive, fearless action wins oftener than any other. The very audaciousness and boldness of the act sometimes confuses and paralyzes the enemy beyond successful effort at resistance. I have no doubt that some of our lives would have paid the penalty of our attempt at escape, and not one of us might have, succeeded in gaining our liberty, yet, if all, of us could have foreseen the final outcome, we could scarcely have made the matter worse by a bold attempt to get out, even if it did cost life.

Finally, after weary days of vain hope to hear something favorable, we set a night for a determined strike for liberty. But it so happened that on the very day of our proposed night escape, an order came for twelve of our number to be sent to Knoxville. The order did not designate by name those who were to go. It merely said twelve of us. The officer handed the order to George D. Wilson, who happened to be down in the yard, where he was allowed, on accout of his being sick that day with cholera-morbus or some ailment of the kind, and asked him to fill in the names. Wilson selected all of his own regimental friends (the Second Ohio) first, and afterwards some of his favorite comrades from other regiments, as he still clung to the exchange delusion, and supposed he was doing his friends thus selected a favor. I was not of the number sent away, but this order, taking away twelve of our party, upset our arrangements for an escape for the time being. After shaking hands with our departing comrades, we were compelled to change our calculations, although we did not abandon the fixed purpose of getting our liberty in *some* way.

One day, some time after this, as we were sitting quietly in our prison, discussing means of escape, an event occurred which hurried matters to a final decision. An officer came in---a stranger to us. After looking at us for a short time, he took from his pocket a paper and handed it to Andrews, then turned and went out without saying a word. Andrews unfolded the paper, glanced at it a moment, and turned away, as if to retire to himself. Poor, ill-fated man! I shall never forget the expression of his countenance as we all fixed our earnest inquiring gaze on him. Not a word was spoken—not a man moved. It was still as death at the hour of midnight. As we exchanged hasty glances with each other, every man seemed to know intuitively the dreadful import of that paper—that it was none other than Andrews' death-warrant. No one ventured to break the dreadful silence, but Andrews passed the paper to us. He was perfectly calm, with no trembling or perceptible emotion, but as we looked upon the paper and read the words, "*and then and there be hanged until he is dead! dead! dead!*" there was not a man of us who did not tremble and show signs of keenest anguish. There was not a man of us who would not have fought to the death for our brave, generous, manly leader. He had, by his noble manhood, bravery and kindness, endeared himself to all. His unselfish regard for every one of the party, his cheerful, quiet, encouraging manner under the most trying ordeals, had caused us to regard him with the greatest confidence and love.

The time fixed in the sentence for his execution gave him just one week longer to live and in which to prepare for death. But we had no idea of using all this precious time in preparing Andrews for death. It was a solemn occasion with us, and all fully realized the awful reality that stared us in the face. This did not mean simply the execution of our noble leader. It was a forerunner of the fate that awaited every man of us.

We now set to work with all the quickened energies of desperate men, bent on escaping or dying in the attempt. Our plan was soon formed. Our old case-knife was called into requisition. The building was of brick, lined with heavy plank. Three men stood on the floor together and the fourth, with the case knife, made into a saw, stood on their shoulders, and was thus enabled to reach the plank ceiling overhead, into which by patience and perseverance we succeeded in sawing a square hole large enough to admit a man's body. We bent ourselves to the task before us both night and day, with a watchman at every window to guard against the discovery of our operations. The noise made by our case-knife saw was effectually drowned by stamping, loud talking, yelling, singing, or anything to keep up a din, and our singers and noise-makers were about as weary with the monotony of their efforts as the saw-shovers.

When two of the planks were so nearly cut out that they could be speedily finished, we filled up the cut so that it could not be noticed easily, and then the fellows below in the "hole," Andrews among them, in the same manner, sawed out notches in the plank which held the bolts of the trap-door. This was discouragingly slow work. The knife-blade would get hot and bend up, and the man who worked it would soon get a tired, blistered hand; but a fresh relay was kept ready, and when the hand of one became too lame to run the saw, he would take his place among the choir of noise-makers, while a fresh man would take the knife.

Old Swims, the jailer, afterwards said he might have known there was some devilment up, the way the d—d Yankees were singing hymns. Singing, however, was a very common pastime with us in the evening, although our best vocalists had gone to Knoxville. Still, although it seems almost like a dream at this distant day, I think we did sing a little longer and louder, on the nights referred to by old Swims, just for the little saw's sake. While this work was going on, others had twisted old blankets and pieces of carpet into ropes, with which to get the men out of the "hole," and by which to descend on the outside.

When everything was in readiness. Andrews, who was to go first, went up in the loft. The work of making a hole out through the brick wall under the roof, was a much more difficult job than we had expected, and proved to be slow work with our case-knife. It had to be done, too, without noise. We at last succeeded in getting out brick enough to allow a man to pass out, just as the grey streaks of dawn began to show in the east. It was nearly daylight. If I remember correctly, each man had his boots or shoes off, so that we could avoid making noise. The blanket rope, one end tied to the rafter, was noiselessly let down the outside wall. We could see the dim gray form of the sentry, and hear his tread as he paced back and forth. It was an anxious moment of suspense, when at last, in a whisper, word was passed from one to the other in the dark prison, that all was ready.

Andrews crept out and swung down, but in some manner a loose brick or piece of mortar fell to the ground and attracted the notice of the sentry and almost instantly we heard the report of a gun. John Wollam, who was next behind Andrews, paid no heed to the shot, but lunged out head over heels. Bang! bang! went the muskets and there was loud shouting —

"Corporal of the guard! Post number—! Captain—Captain of the guard! Halt! Halt!"

Bang! bang! bang! until the shots were as thick as on a skirmish line in a cavalry fight.

The man (Robert Buffum, I think), who was following Wollam through the hole, halted between two

THE PRISON AT CHATTANOOGA.
(The cross indicates the hole above the window on the left side through which Andrews and Wollam escaped.)

opinions, whether he had better jump down while a rebel sentry stood beneath holding a cocked gun with fixed bayonet on him, or crawl back into the old prison cock-loft and bear the ills he was certain of. He crawled back and told us that it was "all up with us." We were all crowded in the loft, waiting for our turn to go out and listening to the racket on the outside. Within a very few moments, almost no time at all, the yard was filled with troops, and by their loud, excited talk we learned, to our unspeakable joy, of the escape of Andrews and Wollam.

The rebels, of course, did not at that moment know who or how many of their prisoners were out, but we in the loft already knew that the excited sentries had fired wildly. At all events, neither Andrews nor Wollam were anywhere to be seen, dead or alive. While we felt the keenest disappointment at our failure to get out, yet we felt a thousand times repaid for our effort that even Andrews had escaped. A heavy load had been lifted from our minds. We took new hope. We knew that Andrews would put forth superhuman efforts to gain the Federal lines, and if he succeeded, we felt certain that Chattanooga would, in all human probability, get a visit very shortly from General Mitchell. We thought if either of the escaped men reached the lines and told our old comrades of our desperate situation, that they would at once demand to be led to our rescue. These were some of the faint rays of hope that gleamed in upon our anxious minds, and in some degree took away the canker of disappointment, somewhat, perhaps, on the same philosophy that says, "A drowning man will catch at a straw," for, indeed, we were basing our hopes on a very slender thread, as the sequel will show.

The musket firing and the news of the jail-break and escape of prisoners spread through camp and town like the wind, and soon the whole population was in a fever of excitement, and all the available man-hunting force, dogs included, joined in the pursuit.

It is hardly necessary for me to tell the reader that those of us who had failed to make good our escape, were now put down in the hole, loaded with heavy irons, and treated with the greatest rigor and severity. This would follow, as a matter of course. This we expected, and were not disappointed. However, we cared nothing for our chains, or the rigor of our treatment, in our great solicitude for the success of Andrews and Wollam. Our anxiety for their safety and successful flight knew no bounds. Hour after hour we passed in sleepless uncertainty and anxious waiting, to catch the first tidings from their pursuers, who were returning from the hunt, and we were overjoyed when we heard that the fugitives had baffled all the skill of both men and dogs. After two days had passed, and still they had not been caught, we began to feel confident. But our rejoicing was of short duration.

As was afterwards learned from Andrews himself, he was fired at by the guard as he scaled the fence outside the prison. But he halted not an instant, and ran rapidly to the river, disrobing himself as he ran. He at once plunged into the Tennessee, and swam for the opposite side. Before he reached the shore, however, the swift current bore him downward, and he became entangled in some driftwood, by which he lost all of his clothing except his coat, and, possibly, his shirt. After reaching the north side of the river he climbed into a tree, where he remained during the entire day, and from which position he was enabled to see his pursuers, and to witness their desperate efforts to find him.

When the friendly shades of night again covered the earth, he cautiously descended from his refuge, and continued his flight in an almost naked and famishing condition. Now, he tore out the arms of his coat, and with these encased his legs as much as he could, so as to afford them some protection against the brush and rocks of that mountainous region. Early in the morning, as he was going across an open field to another tree, for the purpose of shelter during the day, unfortunately, he was discovered, and at once pursued. He dashed forward with the speed of a frightened deer, on, on through the woods, and again to the river, into which he plunged and headed for an island, where he secreted himself among a huge pile of driftwood at the upper end.

Some time during the course of the day a party of searchers, with their blood-hounds, made their appearance, at the sight of which Andrews left his retreat, and made a partial circuit of the island, by wading in the water surrounding it, so as to throw the hounds off his track. After doubling the lower end of the island in this manner, he took refuge in a dense thicket, and again ascended a tree, whose heavy foliage seemed to be an effectual protection from the sight of his relentless pursuers, for, after a long search, they abandoned further pursuit and returned to the main land.

Two lads, however, who had come with the party,

remained behind. In their wanderings on the island, by the merest accident in the world, one of them spied Andrews through an opening in the dense foliage, and at once gave the alarm, when his pursuers returned, and Andrews, seeing that further concealment was at an end, quickly descended, ran to the opposite side of the island, secured a log, and boldly launched into the stream, to make an effort to reach the opposite bank, and thus elude his pursuers. Before he reached the shore, however, he was intercepted by another party in a boat, and was thus completely hemmed in, when he abandoned all further effort to escape and surrendered.

At the prison, we were first startled by a rumor that Andrews had been taken, but were disposed to give little credence to it, probably because we did not desire to believe it. But, alas! the rumor was only too true, for soon after a strong guard of soldiers, having in charge a prisoner, followed by a rabble of citizens, approached the prison. It was Andrews! Oh, how our hearts and hopes sank down within us beyond the power of expression!

Reader, did you ever lose a near and dear friend, and feel that sudden, crushing bereavement, as if all the world had forsaken you, and that a load of sorrow was bearing you down without a helping hand to save or aid you? I have seen those dear to me by ties of kindred called away never to return. I have seen comrades die on the field, and without warning sufficient to speak a parting farewell. I have seen a comrade, endeared to me by long association and friendship amid dangers, chained to me and perishing slowly day by day—his proud spirit broken by disease and hunger, until fever's fitful delirium robbed him of the sense of pain. All of this have I seen and felt, yet God, in His inscrutable ways and infinite mercy, never laid upon me the heavy, chastening hand of sorrow and anguish that I felt when I beheld the brutal guards bringing in poor, ill-fated Andrews, bound hand and foot in heavy chains. I could have prayed that death had spared me those painful moments, the most harrowing of my life.

He was the most wretched, pitiable human being I ever saw—a sight which horrified us all, and even drew words of compassion from some of the prison-guards. His own brother would scarcely have been able to recognize him. It did not seem possible that the short space of three or four days could have wrought a change so startling. As he lay there chained to the floor, naked, bloody, bruised and speechless, he seemed more dead than alive. He had not eaten a morsel since he left us—during which time he had made the most desperate struggle for liberty and life. He had swam about seven miles in the river in his efforts to keep free of the dogs. His feet were literally torn to shreds by running over the sharp stones and through the brush. Toward the last he left blood at every step. He had torn up his coat, all the garment left him, and tied the pieces on his feet, but the protection helped the matter but little. His back and shoulders were sun-blistered almost to the bone, and so completely exhausted and used up was he, that he could barely move his limbs after he was brought in. His face was pale, haggard and emaciated. His eyes, which were sunken, gave forth a wild, despairing, unnatural light.

When we were left alone to ourselves, we drew around the miserable man and, after he had somewhat revived, he told us in that low, calm tone of voice, in which he always spoke and which seldom failed to impress the listener favorably toward the man, the whole story of his unfortunate attempt to escape. He told us he had but little time to live, and that now, after having made every effort to save his life and to rescue us, and failed, he felt reconciled and resigned to his fate. He said he was incapable of doing anything more to help himself, and only regretted that his death could not in some way be instrumental in saving us, his comrades. He counseled us all against the fallacy of hoping for an exchange or for any mercy from those into whose hands we had fallen. He said his doom foreshadowed our own, and entreated us to prepare for the worst, and, when the time came, to prove to them that we were as brave in confronting an ignominious death for our country's sake as we had been fearless in doing service for her. I shall never forget the solemnity of that distressing period of our imprisonment nor the deep impression the words of our poor comrade and leader made on us. Their sad echoings fill my ears now as sensitively as then—almost eighteen years ago—while my utterance chokes and my hand trembles as if that poor, miserable, forlorn man was now before me in the dark prison, speaking words of encouragement and advice.

CHAPTER X.

Our Brave and Noble Leader—His Impending Doom—All Taken to Atlanta Again—Last Advice and Counsel from Andrews—Arrival at Atlanta—Dying the Death of a Spy—The Terrible Tragedy Consummated—Wollam Recaptured after Three Weeks—Account of his Adventures—Mark Wood's Serious Sickness—The Pinchings of Hunger Arrival of our Twelve Comrades from Knoxville—False Hopes--The Old Villain, Thor—A Terrible Blow—Preparing Seven of our Comrades for the Gallows.

"What verse can sing, what prose narrate,
The butcher deeds of bloody fate."

AS I have, since those dark hours, thought over many of the incidents of our two or three months of prison confinement, while Andrews was with us, I can see many reasons for believing that, from the first, he was impressed with a belief that he was never to return from this expedition. He was not by any means a superstitious man, in the sense that word is used, nor was he given to whims, nor did he fear death, yet something in his manner, from the first time I held any conversation with him expressing my concern because we were one day late, leads me to think that he was either a fatalist in belief or that some mysterious, unknown and unaccountable agency whispered to him that he never should return.

He confided to me, and perhaps to several of his comrades, something of his history. He had been a spy, or secret service agent, and made several trips into different parts of the Confederacy, obtaining much useful information, and invariably succeeded in accomplishing whatever he was sent to do. This was, probably, why General Mitchell reposed so much confidence in him as to entrust him as the leader of our expedition. He told me, too, that this was to be his last expedition if he got out alive—that he should never undertake another trip. But, alas, poor fellow, he went once too often.

There was, too, a sad romance connected with Andrews' fate, which I have not reverted too, and which was not, I think, generally known among our band. He was engaged to be married to an amiable, worthy young lady of a highly-esteemed Kentucky family. Whether she knew of the perilous service he was engaged in, I do not know. If she did not, so much heavier must have been the blow to her when she heard of his fate. That he was chivalrously devoted to her I am certain, though it was a subject he seldom alluded to. I am certain, too, that could word have reached her of her lover's perilous situation, that she, through her kinsmen, could have brought strong influences in his favor, though whether his life could have been saved, I very much doubt. Their marriage day had been fixed, and would have taken place a few days previous to the reception of his death sentence. I think this melancholy end of a happy courtship, and the thought of her blighted life, more than anything else, saddened the last days of this heroic man.

A scaffold had already been erected in Chattanooga for the execution of Andrews; but very early on the morning of the day for his execution, we were all taken to the depot and put on the cars for Atlanta. Why this change was so suddenly made in the programme I have never been able to discover. I have two theories. One is, that the mayor and blood-thirsty populace of Atlanta, who had come so near mobbing us, desired to have Andrews and the rest of our party hung in that city, that our blood might, in some manner, appease their bitter wrath. I have heard that the mayor formally made such a request, and have no reason to doubt it, from what I subsequently learned. Again, it will be remembered that Wollam, who broke jail with Andrews, was still at large at the time of which I am speaking, and for all the rebels knew, he might have arrived safely in General Mitchell's lines, and that officer might, at any time, make a dash on Chattanooga and save Andrews' life. It is barely possible, though I think hardly probable, under all the circumstances, that this last was the cause of our sudden removal. We were at a loss to know what this move to Atlanta meant, but it was not worth our while to ask questions.

We were soon whirling along on that same, to us, accursed railroad, for it brought no pleasant memories to us. At each town we were, as before, treated to a deluge of curses, taunts and epithets. Andrews was reminded and taunted at every station of his approaching doom. While we were on the cars, Andrews, who was not chained to any other prisoner, and who sat in the next seat to me, requested me to go into the water closet and leave the window up as high as possible.

Shortly after, Wood and I, who were chained together, went to the closet, and I did my best to open the window high enough for a man's body, but the shutter was so arranged that it could not be raised above six inches. Andrews received the information with a look of sad disappointment. It was his last hope. He did not expect to escape. He would have thrown himself with his chains on from the window when the train was in full motion, and it would have saved them all further trouble with him.

On reaching Atlanta we were conducted to a hall or second-story room, not far from the depot, where we sat down on some benches. We had been here but a short time when a body of soldiers, in charge of several officers, marched up into the building. One of the officers, walking up to Andrews, informed him that the hour for his execution had come, and asked him if he was ready. Andrews replied that he was, only asking the privilege of bidding his comrades farewell.

"Well, then, be d—d quick about it," was the unfeeling reply, "for we have no time to fool away here."

The brave man rose up, and approaching each of us, shook hands and bade us a last farewell. But few of the men could give utterance to a syllable. After this, the doomed man turned and walked away with the officer, and to this day I can hear the clink, clink, clink of those dreadful chains and clogs as, step by step, he descended the stairs. We never saw the noble face and manly form of our leader again.

The reader can better imagine than I can tell, the sorrowful, despondent feelings of our little band. We did not speak words of sorrow. We did not complain,

BIDS HIS COMRADES A FINAL FAREWELL

nor did we shed tears. We had passed that; yet, so bad did we feel for the departed that the terrible silence seemed like a spell kept sacred to his memory.

Soon after, we were ordered down and conducted to the jail of the city, where we were put in iron cages for safe keeping. The guards who came in at ration time in the evening, told us that the tragedy had been consummated; that Andrews died like a brave man. His calmness and noble, manly demeanor shamed even the clamorous mob who were spectators. The limb on which he was hung was so low that his toes touched the ground, and in this way they kept him strangling for a long time, until at last some one took a shovel and mercifully removed the earth, when he soon after expired. The murder was complete.

Thus did J. J. Andrews die the ignominious death of a spy—as noble, as true, as brave a man as ever lifted a hand in defence of our starry flag. He was thirty-two years of age, in the prime and vigor of young manhood. She, who now would have been a happy wife in the love of such a noble, chivalrous man, was left in sorrow and mourning for one whose last moments she could not comfort by her presence, and whose last resting place she should never know.

Let me now turn from this sad episode and, with the reader's kind indulgence, give an account of John Wollam, who was last seen by us as he clambered out of the hole in the jail-loft at Chattanooga, amid the aroused guards. The reader will feel interested to know more of the daring fellow, who risked so much to get away; besides, his success or failure would, we then supposed, have much to do with our subsequent fate. Wollam and Andrews separated instantly on clearing the jail inclosure. Wollam soon reached the river, and finding no way to cross, hit on the happy expedient of making believe that he had crossed. He threw off his coat and vest near the water's edge, walked into the water and waded up the stream a short distance and came out in such a manner as to leave no trace. This ruse worked well. The pursuers, coming to this place, took up their dogs and changed the hunt to the other side of the river. They, of course, failed to find him, and Wollam, who was secreted in a dense thicket not far away, had the satisfaction of seeing them abandon further pursuit. When night came, he left his hiding place, passed around the town on the same side, and a short distance below found a canoe, with which he journeyed down the river by night. He would sink the boat by filling it with stones just before day break, and secrete himself in the brush until night came again.

In this way he worked his way down the Tennessee until he was about eighty miles from Chattanooga, passing Mitchell's extemporised gunboat several times. This was a little steamer which that enterprising officer had captured and fitted up for patrol duty on the Tennessee above and below his camp. Had it been daylight instead of night that Wollam traveled, he would readily have detected the difference, but, as it was, he viewed the craft with suspicion and fear and kept out of sight, by putting in to shore under cover, as she passed. At last, after he had reached a considerable distance down, he began to travel in the day time, which was a fatal mistake. He was spied by a band of rebel cavalry and captured almost within hailing distance of Mitchell's lines. He tried to make them believe he was a Confederate, but a lieutenant of the party, who had helped to capture him the first time, was present, and recognized Wollam as one of the train-stealers, when he was at once sent to Chattanooga and soon arrived, in irons, and was again imprisoned with us in Atlanta jail, after having had his liberty over three weeks. We were much surprised when he returned, for we felt certain that he had reached the Federal lines, or, in case he had not, that he was dead. It seemed as if fate was against us, and that none of our party were destined to reach our friends and make known our unfortunate condition.

But to return. After we had been in the Atlanta jail a short time, the prison-keeper had our chains and hand-cuffs taken off, thinking, no doubt, that between the iron cages in which we were shut at night, the great iron door of the hall and the prison guards, we would be safe. This was a great relief. No one who has worn such incumbrances can realize what a grateful change it made in our situation. We had worn them so long in couples that we would find ourselves involuntarily, at times, following each other about as if still compelled to do so with chains.

My chain-mate, Mark Wood, had been very sick with fever, the result of severe exposure and the confinement and bad treatment in prison. It seemed for a time that he would never get up again. We did all we could for the poor fellow, whose mind was in a delirium, while his body was but a skeleton. After much coaxing and pleading on our part, a doctor was sent in, who administered medicine, and after the fever had taken its course, I had the satisfaction of seeing him change for the better. I sometimes thought that, perhaps, we would do but a merciful kindness to let him die of disease, and thus, possibly, save him from a worse fate; but Wood seemed nearer to me than any other, not only because we were from the same company and regiment, but from our association in the trying days and nights while we were fugitives in the mountains. He seemed to regard me more in the light of a guardian and protector, and relied upon me more than upon himself. This did not make him the most useful comrade in a close emergency, for he did not seem to consider himself capable of acting without first consulting me. Mark was an Englishman by birth, with whom I had no acquaintance before our enlistment. Before entering the service he lived at Portage, and was in the employ of Austin Van Blarcum. He was also in the employ of William Wakefield, of Bowling Green, for some time. He was twenty-one years of age, a bright, free, thoughtless, rollicking Englishman; good humored, impulsive, generous and brave, and had much of the spirit of adventure in his composition, so characteristic of his countrymen. His gratitude toward me, to whom he attributed the saving of his life, never ceased to his dying breath. And, on my part, I may say, perhaps, as truthfully of poor unfortunate Mark, that at the critical moment in my life, he came to my rescue, and by speaking a word in the nick of time saved me, which circumstance will appear further on.

When Mark began to get better, the prisoners would rally him occasionally by saying to him:

"Mark, if I were you, I would not try to get well. You can, by dying, save the rebels the trouble of hanging you. Why not be a little accommodating, since all they do for us is done without pay?"

This, certainly, was not much encouragement to a sick man, yet Mark would laugh a wild, unnatural laugh, and say he was going to get well to spite them.

We passed the time, some playing checkers or cards if they had them, singing, reading the Scriptures or almost anything that we could get to read, in discussions and in various ways such as are known to those who have been in prison. At best, prison life is a dreary, monotonous, tiresome existence. Some circumstances in our case made it especially so. The rations we received at this prison were both scanty, and, at times, loathsome, and for Wood, our invalid comrade, I feared they would cause his death, even after he could walk about, for he had a ravenous appetite and would devour the scanty allowance of coarse corn-bread, ground cob and all, with his bit of spoiled bacon—which stunk sometimes beyond the endurance of a well man—like a wolf, and scarcely stop to pick out the worms that had been boiled with it.

Sometimes, in the absence of corn-bread, we would get a few negro peas, which were boiled with the meat, and these peas were infested with little bugs, which, with the maggots in the meat, were almost enough to convulse the stomach of a hungry dog. I have found, by experience, and I think I will be corroborated by all the men who have been in rebel prisons and suffered the protracted pangs of hunger and starvation, that man, when forced to it, is as ravenous, reckless, unreasonable and brutish in his appetite as the lowest order of animal creation. In Andersonville, history tells us that men murdered and robbed their own comrades in order that they might sell their few effects to the guards for bread. In one of the Richmond prisons I have heard tell of two brothers, almost crazy from the pangs of hunger, fighting brutally over a miserable little mouthful of the flesh of a dog. Hunger knows no arbitrary law nor code of honor.

While time hung thus heavily, we were surprised one day to hear that the balance of our party had arrived. These were the twelve men who had been sent to Knoxville for trial, and of whose fate we had since been ignorant. They, with some Tennessee Unionists, had been put in a room in the back part of the jail in which we were imprisoned. The next day two or three of them obtained permission from the guard to come into our room. From them we learned that seven of their number had been tried by court-martial, but none of them knew what the decision was.

About this time, and before any more could be tried, events occurred in other quarters that caused the court-martial to break up and the officers to hurry to their respective commands. I suppose this was caused by the capture of Cumberland Gap by General Morgan and the threatened invasion of East Tennessee by the Federals, or, perhaps, the officers were needed to go with Bragg on his great raid into Kentucky.

Our comrades all seemed in good spirits and hopeful. They had heard of the death of Andrews before they left Knoxville. They had also been told by some of the guard that Andrews was the only man intended to be executed, and that the rest of us would simply be kept until the war was over. This gave much encouragement to some of our men, but I must confess I was not in a frame of mind to build much hope on these reports. The admonition of Andrews still rang in my ears. There seemed to exist a feeling of fiendish, malicious brutality toward us, that was felt and shown toward no other prisoners except the East Tennessee Union men, whose wrongs and sufferings during the war have been so graphically portrayed by Parson Brownlow.

For instance, our comrades who had just arrived, told us that as they reached the depot in Atlanta, they were taunted and jeered by the mob, and a man, who said he was the mayor, told them he should have the pleasure of putting the rope on each of their necks, as he had done to their miserable, thieving, spying scoundrel of a leader, Andrews. He told them they would not be troubled with any more railroad rides. Again, the jailer, whom I have since visited, when I was free and wore the blue, was a humane man, and at first gave us liberal rations. He was soon suspected of being too friendly with us, and this duty taken out of his hands, and an odious, wretched old Yankee-hater, named Thor, who was a fit instrument for the business, was hired as a spy on the jailer's actions.

I will here give it as my best impression that Thor, the old villain, met his just deserts when Sherman's men captured Atlanta. There were six men in that vast army of veteran fighters, who had been victims to the old miscreant's cruelty and hatred of Yankees.

This whole matter of doubt and uncertainty was soon

set at rest, for one afternoon, about a week after the arrival of our Knoxville comrades, a body of cavalry, in charge of officers, filed in and halted in front of the jail. Several of the officers and a strong guard of men came up and halted in front of our room. Our party, at this time, had arranged so that we had all been allowed in a room together during the day. We knew then there was something up. Soon the door opened, and the officer read off the names of our comrades who had been tried at Knoxville. They were as follows:

Samuel Robinson, John Scott, Perry G. Shadrack, Samuel Slavens, William Campbell, Marion Ross and George D. Wilson.

One of the men, Robinson, was sick with fever, and had to be assisted to his feet and out of the room. He was abused by the officers shamefully. They were taken to a room near by, occupied by the Tennessee prisoners, and the latter were brought over and put into our room. There was much excitement and speculation on our part. With bated breath we eagerly inquired of each other what this could all mean. Some even supposed our comrades had been taken out to be paroled or exchanged.

The room into which they were taken was only separated from ours by a hall, and we could hear the doom of the poor fellows pronounced as their death sentences were read to them, and they were enjoined to hurry up and get ready to accompany the guard to the place of execution, as time was precious, and they had no moments to waste. The whole party at once returned to our room, and George D. Wilson, with pale face and quivering lip, informed us in a startling whisper, that they were to be hung immediately. Even while our doomed comrades were saying their farewells to us, the rebel guards were busily engaged in pinioning their arms with ropes, preparatory to their journey to the scaffold. Their relentless executioners drove them in impatient, brutal haste, even refusing them the poor boon of saying farewell to some of their comrades.

That terrible moment will never be effaced from the tablets of my memory. It is indelibly and vividly engraven there. It was a sudden and dreadful blow to those poor fellows, who had been lured into the false hope of being exchanged or paroled. From the very instant the cavalry halted in front of our prison, an unexplainable horror had seized upon me. I felt that their visit meant no good to us, and when the epauletted brute, who had charge of the murderers, came in and informed us who were left in the room, that they would attend to the rest of us very soon, I felt almost like thanking him for saying so, for there would be no more doubting. We knew exactly what to expect and could act accordingly. Then came the choking, hurried farewells. Oh, what a sad, sad, trying moment that was! It is as vividly before me now as then, and the last farewell of those dear comrades, as they left us, will linger and pain me as long as consciousness remains.

CHAPTER XI.

Painful Reflections—Brave Bearing of the Doomed Seven—"Tell Them I Died for My Country"—Poor John Scott—George Wilson's Dying Speech on the Gallows—A Brutal Scene—Rope Breaks with Two—It is Readjusted and the Tragedy is Complete—Seven Murdered Heroes—Southern Barbarity—An Afternoon Never to be Forgotten—Solemn Hours in Prison—Sacred to the Memory of Our Comrades—A Night of Prayer—Captain David Fry—A Christian Hero—A Rebel Minister—Letter Sent to Jeff Davis and its Probable Result.

"Our bread was such as captives' tears
Have moisten'd many a thousand years,
Since man first pent his fellow men
Like brutes within an iron den."

THE blow fell with greater weight upon some of the doomed men from the fact they had built such strong hopes of a better fate. It will be remembered as related in a former chapter, that George Wilson and Marion Ross, two of the fated men, now bidding us a final farewell, had been so strongly impressed with this fallacious belief that they had been partly instrumental in preventing an attempt to escape at Chattanooga. But, oh! how terribly were they and all of our party undeceived, and how truly prophetic and correct were the warning words of Andrews! How much better than we did he know the frenzied, blood-thirsty, merciless nature of the horde who were waging a war for the perpetuity of human slavery.

The first warning those men had of their doom after they were separated from us was when the officer handed them each a paper containing their death-sentence, and before they had time to read the terrible words the guards were tying their arms with ropes. Robinson, who was so sick with fever that he could not stand on his feet, was cursed and threatened by the officer, by whose orders he was dragged out and down stairs.

The measureless pain and sorrow I felt for the fate of those comrades, is to this day mingled with proud admiration for their noble, manly fortitude in that trying moment. A true man, in the mad excitement of strife on the battle-field, can march with his comrades to meet death without faltering, but for an innocent man to bravely and calmly meet the fate of a murderer on the scaffold, is a test of courage for a soldier, which few men can realize until commanded to prepare for the halter. It is hard for a man in the full vigor of health and the prime of life to imagine what his feelings would be, if called upon suddenly to face an ignominious fate at the hands of exultant, heartless executioners, and in the presence of a blood-thirsty, jeering rabble, and without so much as a half-hours time to arrange his spiritual and temporal affairs; yet such was the lot of our comrades, and they met their fate like true soldiers.

Marion Ross was the least affected. As he shook hands with us, he spoke out in a clear tone of voice and said: "Boys, if any of you ever get back, tell them I died for my country; tell them I died like a man and did not regret it." Our party seemed to be like the majority of young men who entered the army—careless of any preparations or thought for the world beyond the grave.

George Wilson, who had one of the brightest minds of the party, was a professed disbeliever—an infidel, and often I had heard him argue with William Pittenger against the truth of the Scriptures while in prison. Pittenger, I believe, was intending to engage in the ministry. In this last, solemn moment, however, Wilson took Pittenger by the hand and said, "I believe you are right, Pittenger. Oh, try to prepare for death better than I have done. May God bless you—farewell."

Slavens, who was a man athletic of stature and Herculean in strength, and would have been a fit soldier for the days and army of Frederick the Great, could only articulate to his near friend, Buffum, "Wife—children—tell—them—" when his utterance choked, and he completely broke down.

There was one of that fated band whose parting farewell is painfully vivid before me to-day—a member of my own proud and honored regiment, the Twenty-First Ohio—John Scott, as brave, faithful and patriotic a son, brother and husband as ever shouldered a musket for his country. Alas! little did he think, when three days after his marriage to a worthy young lady of his native town, he parted from her, of the fate that awaited him, and little did that patriotic and loving bride dream that the young husband she had surrendered up to his country's call must die the death of a martyr on the scaffold! John Scott was from Findlay,

Ohio, and was one of the best men in our party. He was a good soldier, quiet, determined, persevering and brave. He bore all his deprivations and hardships with manly fortitude, and, as he came to each of us for the last time, he clasped our hands in silent agony. No tears—no words. His noble breast did not throb for fear of death, although his executioners stood all about him, but for those he loved so dearly, that he was never to see again. I have, since the war, visited his family and friends in his once happy home, where the memory of the noble son and brother is still cherished and mourned; and which sorrow is shared in by every survivor of that little band of men.

Our comrades were hauled from the prison to the place of execution in an old wagon. The scenes that transpired there we learned from our guards the same evening, or the following day. As near as we could get at the facts, as related by them, the scaffold was surrounded by about five hundred guerrillas, or bush-whacking cavalrymen, who, probably, had never been near enough to the Federal lines to smell gunpowder or blood. These rangers, or guerrillas, disputed for the honor of becoming the murderers, and finally twelve were selected by vote. When the doomed men were on the scaffold, in the presence of that excited, jeering mob, George Wilson, who was game to the last and worthy a better fate, asked permission to say a few words. Out of curiosity, perhaps, on their part, he was allowed to speak. His words, most likely, disappointed them, still they listened, while one of those "terrible, thieving, cowardly Yankees" stood up there on that trap-door of death and in a calm, unfaltering voice spoke earnest words of wisdom and warning to them. His calmness and deliberation and his clear voice commanded their attention and his words seemed to awe the desperate, blood-thirsty rabble into silence. He told them that they were doing wrong in rebelling against their government—that they had been misguided by their leaders and that they would soon have cause to regret the course they were taking. He earnestly admonished them that the old Union would be restored and that the old flag would again float over their city. He told them that, although condemned as a spy, yet he was not a spy and they well knew it. He was only a soldier performing a duty for which he had been detailed. He told them he did not fear nor regret to die, but only regretted the manner of his death.

His words made a deep impression on the crowd. Many of them evidently thought that if the Yankee army was all of his mind and bravery the probabilities were that the Union *would* be restored and the rebellion squelched.

When Wilson ceased speaking the signal was given and the trap was sprung. Two of the men, Campbell and Slavens, who were very heavy, broke their ropes and fell to the ground insensible. When they came to a little, they asked for water and also requested a little time for prayer. The water was given them, and they were allowed to live long enough to see the lifeless bodies of their comrades placed in coffins, when they were peremptorily ordered to reascend the scaffold, when the ropes were soon adjusted and the two men again launched off, this time into an unknown eternity.

Thus were those seven men murdered, without warning—without a friend to say a last encouraging, sympathetic word—without a spiritual adviser—yes, without the last poor privilege of a little time to offer up for themselves an humble petition to the Throne of Grace, for a merciful Savior to receive their souls, where suffering and sorrow are at an end. It seemed as if the heartless fiends sought to murder both body and soul. The blackest-hearted criminal is always allowed, in civilized nations, the consolation of spiritual advice and prayer; but these, our poor, unfortunate comrades, who were guilty of no crime other than trying to serve their country, were sent before their Creator without even so much as the privilege accorded a common criminal. Yet these same unchristian men—rebels—the leaders in the government and society who thus brutally treated the soldiers of this great government, are to-day seeking place and power in the nation they sought to destroy, and in doing which they took a fiendish, delight in heaping the most inhuman tortures that their innate cruelty could devise upon those who came to its defense in the hour of its danger. Was ever a government so merciful and lenient to its enemies? I think there is no parallel to it in history. I ask the reader's pardon for this digression.

We learned, also, that the rebel soldiers, after the execution, spent the remainder of the day and evening in drunken revelry and jollification, because of the seven "Yanks" they had had the pleasure of putting out of the way, and with a further prospect of soon having another hanging-bee for the "Yanks" yet left in jail. The reader can well imagine the scene of sorrow and utter desolation which reigned among us who were left in that gloomy prison.

That afternoon and evening will never be forgotten by those of us who were confined within those hated walls. We were bowed with a grief too oppressive for words. Each one bore the bitterness of those hours in close communion with himself. No pen can describe the anguish of those moments. All joviality was at an end—no word of consolation was uttered—not a gleam of hope seemed to illumine those dark and terrible hours, as they dragged so slowly along. How long that dark pall of gloom surrounded us, with a silence that was terrible, I know not. Some one, at last, suggested prayer, and every member of our remaining little band bowed in compliance with that suggestion.

That prayer meeting was one of the most solemn and impressive ever witnessed. It was led by Captain David Fry, an East Tennesseean, who had been brought with the twelve of our party from the court-martial at Knoxville, and after our seven comrades had been led out to execution, he was placed in the room with us. For some time those devotional exercises were continued, and this good, brave and loyal man proved himself no less worthy as a spiritual adviser, than he was a trusty leader against the schemes of rebel foes.

Captain Fry, who ever after stood by us with such fortitude that we all learned to love him, belonged to a Union regiment in East Tennessee, and was held as a spy and bridge-burner—a charge very similar to that brought against us—although he was captured when fighting bravely at the head of his column, and covered with wounds. He was one of the best and noblest hearted men I ever met—a soldier and a patriot—a Christian and a gentleman. His influence had been a power in behalf of the Union in East Tennessee. He first came to notice by some feats of daring, and, I think, is mentioned prominently in the book published by Dan. Ellis, the famous Tennessee scout and spy. Captain Fry first saw service in the Mexican war, and was a man of fine stature and great muscular power—brave as a lion, yet tender and sympathetic as a child to those in need or distress. He organized a company of his Union neighbors, and led them through the mountains to Kentucky. On the assurance of help by the Union Generals in Kentucky, he consented to make a trip back to East Tennessee, for the purpose of destroying important lines of railroad communication, and rallying the Union men. It was an arduous and dangerous undertaking. Had he been promptly helped, as seemed possible at that time, he would have saved much of the suffering and persecution endured by the people of that State, and given a strong element to the Union cause, which was murdered, driven off, or forced into the rebel army or prisons. As it was, he was left to his fate almost unaided. The rebels concentrated a strong armed force, and while Fry was conducting a body of Union refugees to Kentucky, he was attacked by a superior force, and, after a brave fight, he was wounded and captured, and had the daily assurance from his captors that he would quit this world at the end of a rope—an assurance he had no reason to doubt the ultimate fulfillment of. He was of inestimable value to our little forlorn band, and was a good man in a "close emergency," as will be seen hereafter.

As has been previously mentioned, only eight of our party, including Andrews, had gone through the form of a trial; but at one time during our stay at Chattanooga when our hopes were quite high, that we should be paroled or exchanged like other prisoners, most of the men had consented that after two or three had been tried, the rest would accept the verdict adjudged by the court, and abide the decision the same as if all had been tried. We could see no reason why there should be any difference in the verdict in each case, except for Andrews, and, possibly Brown, the engineer, in case they found him. out. Afterwards this looked like a trap, into which we had been drawn, when we had been led to hope for lenient treatment.

It will be readily observed that we were now in a state of doubt and suspense well nigh intolerable. Neither could we get any information as to how or when we were to be disposed of. We had no friend, no lawyer, no counselor, and from day to day groped along in this wearing, trying uncertainty. We had not been tried, nor had we any reason to believe that they intended to give us a trial, yet, why had they not executed us with the rest of our comrades, who were guilty of no greater or less offence than ourselves? We watched every movement and word that was spoken, to learn, if possible, what the next step in our cases would probably be. Of their intention to execute us we had no doubt. Thus time dragged on week after week. We resorted to every kind of amusement we could think of to keep our minds from getting into a state of despondency. Card-playing we had banished from our midst since the execution of our comrades, but we played checkers on a board cut on the floor, engaged in discussions, talked about the war, its final outcome, its results upon the country, what would be done with the rebels, their property, etc., etc.

While we were dragging out this miserable, monotonous existence, providentially or otherwise, a preacher of the city, named McDonald, a Presbyterian I believe, visited us one day. He was a friendly, kind-hearted man, and, I believe, a true Christian, although I noticed, when we all kneeled in prayer at his request, after we had joined him in singing a hymn, he opened his prayer with the singular petition that our lives might be spared *if it was in accordance with the best interests of the Confederacy.* This prayer did not suit us exactly, but we felt that this kind man's voice would, in the end, have little weight in the scale, for or against our lives, so far as the Confederates were concerned, for they were an ungodly set at best. If this good man is yet living, he has my best wishes, as being the only rebel, besides our old jailer, who ever spoke a kind, encouraging word to me during all my imprisonment and fugitive wanderings in that slave-cursed land. He afterwards loaned us a few books, such as "Bunyan's Pilgrim's Progress," "Milton's Paradise Lost," etc., which one of our company would read aloud, while the rest maintained the best of order. This was a great comfort to us and kept our minds from brooding over our heavy burden of woe. As each day would fade into night, and the long, red rays of the setting sun gleam through the prison bars, we would wonder if we might ever see its fading glory again. We remembered constantly that each day might be our last. We had almost ceased to even hope to see our friends again, who lived in what our boys called "God's country." Our thoughts would wander away to them, and many a time a silent tear might be seen to course its way unbidden down the cheek of some poor fellow who had not spoken for an hour. Our food was so scanty and bad as to keep us on the verge of starvation and to crush all the spirit and resolution we had. We wondered, as the weeks rolled by, why we were not executed—why they still kept us.

Finally, we conceived the notion to write to Jeff. Davis, himself, the boss traitor and leading spirit of the wicked rebellion. We were certain that it could not make our condition any worse. Some of our party occasionally would sell a vest or some other garment to the rebel guards for a little scrip, and in this way we could get trifles, such as a bit of tobacco and the like, and I suppose it was in this way we procured paper and material to write to Davis. Mr. Pittenger, an intelligent man in our party, acted as scribe, and a respectful letter, setting forth our condition as well as we could, was written, sealed, stamped and directed properly to the rebel chief, at Richmond, and through a little good management by the negro cook, who took the letter to the postoffice, 1 have every reason to believe it reached its destination.

We never heard anything from it, but we did hear a short time afterward that the Provost Marshal of Atlanta got a sharp letter from the rebel Secretary of War, wanting to know "why in h—l those train-thieves had not been executed," evidently having been under the impression that we had all been hung long since.

The Provost referred the Secretary to the record of proceedings of the Knoxville court-martial. Whether our letter had anything to do in the premises we never knew, but we became aware that there was some pretty pointed correspondence going on between Colonel Lee, the Provost, and the Richmond authorities, and that we had reason to feel deeply concerned, the reader may infer, from the fact that we set about taking desperate measures to once more try to escape.

CHAPTER XII.

The Jail at Atlanta—Preparations to Break Jail—Expecting an Order for Our Execution—We Must Strike a Blow for Liberty—The Plan Determined—Busy Preparations—Prayer for Deliverance—The Last Desperate Chance—The Critical Moment—The Blow is Struck—Fighting the Guards—Away We Go—Liberty, Once More—The Pursuit.

> "There is a war, a chaos of the mind,
> When all its elements convulsed—combined—
> Lie dark and jarring with perturbed force."

IN order that the reader may more fully understand that which will be detailed hereafter, I will briefly describe the jail in which we were confined. The building, the walls of which were of brick, and very thick, was a pretty large one, enclosed by a high, tight board fence, similar to most prisons. In front of the jail there was a heavy door or gate that opened through the fence into the jail yard, and by which ingress and egress to and from the jail was had. This gate was usually kept locked; besides, a sentry was kept on duty, and sometimes two, at this entrance. The jail, which was two stories high, had several rooms below, used for the convenience of the jailer and his family. There was a hall that led clear through the building, from the front door to a door which led into the back yard. A stairs led up from the right hand side of the hall, a few paces from the front door, to a similar hall in the second story. On each side of the second story hall were two large rooms, and in two of these rooms was a stout iron cage, similar to that which Barnum used to carry the big rhinoceros in. That they were built strong, I know from experience, and also that there was no chance to get out of a cage unless with assistance from the outside. In the rear of these cage-rooms, and in the back part of the building, were two rooms without cages. Each of these rooms had two windows, strongly barred across with iron. Besides the brick walls which surrounded the four sides of every room, there was a second wall inside of the brick and fastened to it, of oak plank laid one upon the other flat and thoroughly spiked through and through. Every door was strongly built of heavy iron bars riveted together, and hung on massive hinges. From this imperfect description of our prison, the reader will see that the prospect of our *breaking* out was not the best. In vain had we looked and examined and re-examined these walls to find a weak spot that promised us the least hope for once more gaining our liberty.

But the evidences were increasing daily that there was "something in the wind" that boded no good to us. We resolved unanimously—a resolve that may seem to the reader on a par with the resolution of the convention of mice in the fable, that resolved to put a bell on the cat—to *get out* if—if—we became satisfied that we were to be executed. The negro cooks, also the jailer's wife and daughters, were not in sympathy with the rebellion. Neither do I believe the jailer was a rebel at heart, yet so closely was he watched that he dared not show any friendship toward us. Still, we managed to get much information through these sources, although it was impossible that they could afford us any substantial assistance.

We communicated with the prisoners in the room opposite to us through the stove-pipe, which entered the same chimney from both rooms, the pipe-holes being almost exactly opposite. We would take off the pipe-elbow and speak through, tube fashion, though we had to be careful that we were not overheard. It was by this means that we learned, from some new prisoners brought in, of the Emancipation Proclamation of President Lincoln. This caused great commotion among the rebels, and brought down bitter maledictions upon the good President Lincoln's head. The negroes, ignorant as they were, seemed to take a lively interest in the Proclamation, and were never so pleased as when they could speak to us on the sly about it.

About this same time, a couple of regular army soldiers, confined in the next room, which overlooked the front yard, overheard Colonel Lee, the Provost, telling the officer of the guard that he hourly expected an order for the execution of "those raiders." This information was soon made known to us, and only corroborated other reports that we had heard, and things that we had seen. The day following, the wife of a citizen prisoner came in to visit her husband, and she told him that it was the general talk in the city that the Yankee raiders were to be executed within a day or two, and that everybody was going to witness the execution. This man sent word to us as soon as he could from his room, and further advised us to try to break jail. He did not know that we had already decided to do so, for we kept our plans entirely secret.

After sifting and weighing closely all the information we had, it stood about in this way: The rebel Secretary of War had issued orders to the commander of that department that we should be executed without further delay, and a little formality—Confederate army red tape—was all that now stood between us and the scaffold. This would not save our necks long. It might be an hour; it might be as long as a week; but, if we had any hope of getting beyond those prison walls, except on a death-cart to the gallows, the blow must be struck at once. Otherwise we might as well say our prayers and resign ourselves to our fate.

I believe in the efficacy of earnest Christian prayer, but prayer in a Confederate prison seemed to have less effect than in any place I have ever before or since been, and had it not been for the kind preacher who visited us in jail, I should feel like giving it as my belief that God, in His anger, had stricken that part of rebeldom from Heaven's court calender, as unworthy of representation in His kingdom of peace, justice and good will, and only fit for the fare of Sodom and Gomorrah.

We resolved to make the attempt to regain our liberty and save our lives without further delay. Hazardous and unpromising as was the prospect, it could not result in worse than death, and that was our fate in any event within a day or two. Our plan was quickly agreed upon. We had talked the matter over hundreds of times of late. It was not to break the jail, for that, as is already known, was an impossibility with our poor means in the way of implements.

We had decided to seize the jailer, Mr. Turner, when he came to the door to put in our rations, take the keys from him, unlock the doors and let out the prisoners in the other rooms, then all descend the stairs, and divide into two squads—one squad to go to the rear door and capture the guards, while the other squad should capture and disarm the guards at the front door and in the yard. This was all to be done as quietly as possible. Then, with the muskets so obtained, we might be able to march on the double quick out of the city, at once scatter to the nearest woods, and make the best disposal of ourselves that circumstances would admit of.

When it is remembered that we were in the jail of a large city, not a street of which we knew, that soldiers, home guards and police could be rallied at a moment's warning, and that the whole population, dogs and all, would freely turn out to hunt for the train-thieves, and the further fact that we had been so reduced and enfeebled by months of confinement and hunger, that we were but shadows of our former selves, and it will be seen that we had no small contract on our hands. But experience has taught me that man, in the fix we were, is the worst and most desperate creature on earth, and will do things that seem utter impossibilities before their accomplishment.

We at once set about preparing ourselves for a journey. We mended our old, worn-out clothes as well as we could, so that our appearance among strangers would not betray us. We cut out old pieces of blankets and made socks to protect our feet from our old, worn, hard shoes and boots. We gathered up several hickory sticks that we had in prison, and also some old bottles and such other implements that we could lay hands on, to use as weapons in our assault on the guards. The time fixed for the assault was in the evening when our supper rations were brought in, which was sometime before sunset, and when our movements outside, should we succeed, would soon be covered by darkness. The routes to be taken after we were out were discussed and it was agreed by all that we must avoid any of the principal roads or ferries of the surrounding country.

Captain Fry engaged the party in prayer for our safe deliverance, and a few moments before ration time came, we all shook hands and bid each other good bye, many of the men shedding tears, for we knew and felt that we should never all meet again in this world. Captain Fry shed tears like a child. I can distinctly see that noble head, whose locks were sprinkled a little with iron gray, as on bended knees, he prayed for our deliverance, and as tremulously he shook our hands at the parting. It was decided not to make the attempt when the rations were passed in to us, but to wait until the door was opened the second time, after we had had time to eat, for the purpose of taking out the ration-pan or bucket and giving us water. This would make the time so much nearer sundown or dark, which was very important to us.

When the door was opened, we were in our usual places, and tried to look as composed as possible, as the negro came in and set down our "feed," while the jailer held the door and looked in through the bars. The door was closed after the negro went out and into the other rooms. Had the jailer scrutinized closely, I think he could have seen that something unusual had, or was about to transpire, for a settled look of determination and desperate resolve was set in every man's eye and face, and to me, at least, was plainly visible. Most of the men, while pretending to eat their rations, quietly bid away a morsel in their pockets for the morrow.

Each man had his part assigned him, like the players in a drama. Captain Fry had the post of honor. To him, by common consent, was entrusted the "ticklish" job of seizing the jailer at the door, on account of his powerful build and great strength. I can scarcely remember now the details of the work assigned to each man. My own part of the work was with the squad that was to tackle the guards in the front yard. We prolonged the supper ceremony as long as possible, in order to gain time. After some twenty minutes, perhaps, the jailer returned to the door, and putting his bunch of keys down to the great lock, it loosened with a loud click and came out of the staple, when Mr. Turner stood on the threshold.

The critical moment had come.

We were all watching Captain Fry, for the noble man of prayers and tears was a cool-headed, brave soldier as well. He took his position near the door, and, as the jailer stepped in, he placed his hand on his shoulder as if to speak privately with him, and, with a smile as pleasant as a May morning and the courtly obeisance of a cavalier, he threw Mr. Turner entirely off his guard as he said:

"A pleasant evening, Mr. Turner," and reaching his

arm around the jailer's neck, continued, "we have concluded to take a walk—." At this instant he clapped his hand over Turner's mouth, suppressing that man's half-uttered call for the guard, and held the surprised and struggling jailer as if in a vice. Robert Buffum, at the same time, sprang like a cat, and with a single surge, wrenched the bunch of keys from the jailer's hand. Turner was a stout, wiry man, and struggled violently, but Fry held him with the powerful embrace of a "grizzly," while a steady hand over his mouth and neck kept him from making any alarm, Fry at the same time cautioning him to keep quiet—that he would not be hurt.

Buffum, in the meantime, keys in hand, was slinging the doors open right and left, and, in less time than I am telling it, all the prisoners who wanted to *go* were marshaled in the hall and ready for a descent on the guards below. Luckily for old Thor, he was not about; if he had been, a glass bottle on the head would have been his portion. To go to the yard, front and rear, was but the work of an instant.

The guards were thunderstruck with surprise, and were disarmed before they recovered their senses, except three cowardly sand-lappers, who ran out of the gate screaming, "Murder! Corporal of the guard! Captain of the guard! Police! Murder!" and other exclamations of alarm.

After yelling themselves nearly hoarse, they took refuge behind the fence, outside of the gate, and pointed their muskets inside. Several of the guards had been knocked down and roughly handled. One fellow, more combative than some of his comrades, brought his mus-

11

ket to a guard and showed fight, but one of our party knocked him cold with a heavy bottle. The cowardly yelpers, who had ran to the gate and given the alarm, had spoiled our arrangements for getting away to the woods quietly, but I did not realize this at the time, so intent was I in performing my part at the front gate.

I ran to a pile of loose brick, near the corner of the jail, and arming myself with these I ran for the fellows at the gate. They would dodge back when I would throw at them. I must have hurt one of them severely, and whether I had any assistance from any of our party I cannot tell. I know I kept calling and waiting for them to come on, when, suddenly, I heard a familiar voice call my name.

"Alf, come on, quick! the boys are getting over the fence at the back of the jail; hurry up, for God's sake, for there's a company of guards coming double quick.

This was my old comrade, Mark Wood, and his voice was the first warning I had of the danger that threatened me, or of the necessary change in our programme.

"Then bounce that fence," I yelled to Mark, and, dropping my brick-bats, I also sprang for the fence, my feet scarcely touching the ground. We both reached the top of the high fence at the same instant, and not a second too soon, for as I glanced over my shoulder from the fence-top, I saw the guards with gleaming muskets pouring in at the gate, and before I could throw my leg over and spring off, a volley was fired, the balls rattling and whizzing all about us. One bullet struck the picket under my thigh, and so close that the

RACING FOR THE WOODS.

splinters lacerated my flesh, and as my feet struck the ground on the outside, I said to Mark, “I am hit.”

“Get up and run like h—l, then!” exclaimed Mark.

I was on my feet in an instant, not knowing whether my thigh was shattered or not. As I ran I clapped my hand there to see if it bled freely. I pulled away a lot of splinters, and had the satisfaction of finding that I had received only a slight flesh wound made by the picket splinters. Never, did I make better use of my legs; there was need of it, too, for the balls were spatting about us in the dirt uncomfortably near. They came so thick and closely at one time that I was almost certain that one or both of us would be hit; but we answered their cries of “Halt! halt!” by springing forward with all the speed we could command.

After having run a long distance in our flight, we passed Buffum, who had lost his hat in the attack, and, now, bareheaded and with his eyes fairly starting out of his head with exertion, the poor fellow looked the very picture of a wild man. Wood had fallen behind me in the race, and I could hear Buffum cheering and urging him to “pull into it” for dear life. “I can’t run, but I can stop them! Run, Wood! Keep on running, and never let up!” Thus the brave fellow, completely fagged out, encouraged my partner, who still felt and showed the effects of his sickness. I was far enough ahead so that I had time to select the most favorable course for us to take to save distance and find the shelter of woods or thickets.

It was about a mile before we struck the cover of woods, and then the trees were so scattering that they afforded only a doubtful place for concealment. It was now every man for himself, and, like the Duke of Wellington at Waterloo, we longed for darkness or some other friendly interposition in our behalf. Wood had come up with me, and we dodged stealthily from one thicket to another until it began to grow quite dark, when we breathed easier and acted more deliberately, although we well knew we were not out of danger yet.

About this time, we became aware that we were approaching a public road. We soon had warning that it was much better to halt, and not attempt to cross the road. The sound of galloping horsemen in great numbers and the clanking of sabers could be heard near by. We were so nearly out of breath that we could run no farther for the present, and, on looking hastily about, we discovered a low, scrubby pine bush surrounded with shrubbery. We both darted under its protecting shelter and lay flat on the ground on our faces, neither having spoken a word to the other for some minutes, on account of our great exhaustion. We were so near the road that we could plainly see all the movements of the rebel cavalry, who were deploying their line something in the manner of skirmishers.

This presented an unexpected difficulty in our way. If we had reached the road two minutes sooner we might have crossed without being seen, but we could not have been there an instant sooner than we were, unless we had had wings, for we had both run until we were ready to fall in our tracks. We had become separated from the rest of the party, but we could still hear the reports of muskets, and knew that the pursuit was still going on, but how many of the escaping party had been killed was beyond our knowledge, though I had seen Captain Fry reeling and stumbling in a manner that led me to fear he was shot. We were thus compelled to lie quietly for some time. While we were waiting here, the cavalry was relieved by infantry, and the cavalry, as soon as relieved, formed into squads and started to scour the woods.

CHAPTER XIII.

Eluding Pursuit—Crossing the Line of Rebel Guards—Physical Prostration—Discouraging Journey before Us—Paroxysm of Joy—Striking Out for the Gulf—Hungry and Foot-sore—Crouching from the Sight of Men—The Intensity of our Afflictions—Bitter Reflections—On the Verge of Despair—We Reach the Chattahooche, and Hope Springs Up Anew—We Find a Boat and are Soon Gliding Down the River Gulfward.

"Strange — that where Nature lov'd to trace
As if for gods, a dwelling place,
There man, enamor'd of distress,
Should mar it into wilderness."

THE place where we lay was not over fifteen steps from where the infantry sentinel was stationed. We could hear every word he spoke to the man on the next post. Their comments on the affair at the jail would have been amusing to us under less serious circumstances, and I wish I could give their words exactly now, for they were ludicrous enough. In their opinion there was no sort of devilment that a "Yank" was not an adept in, from stealing a "nigger'' or a railroad to breaking a jail, murdering peaceful citizens, and in various other ways defying the regulations and rights of the Southern people. They allowed that old Mitchell had picked out the off-scourings and most reckless jail-breakers and pick-pockets in his army to send out on this thieving business, and that if any of the raiders were caught there would be no more foolish delay about hanging them.

Sometime late in the evening, while we were still lying under the bush, we became aware that some one was approaching us very quietly. In the dark we could recognize the dim outlines of two men, and we felt certain, as they came so near us that we could have almost touched them, that it was two of our comrades; but we dare not even whisper to them lest we should cause them to betray themselves, and, perhaps, us too. They were, evidently, from the cautious manner in which they moved, aware that they were very close to the rebel guards. These men, I afterwards learned, were Porter and Wollam.

After waiting a short time to see if they were discovered, and hearing nothing of them, we began to crawl out, concluding that there was no probability of the guards leaving that night. I should judge the sentries were stationed about thirty paces apart, and to get out, there was no alternative but to pass between them. I selected a place and crawled on my belly to the other side of the road safely, and then lay perfectly still, while Mark did the same. My hair fairly stood on end as he wriggled along, for it seemed to me once or twice as if one of the sentries would certainly discover him before he would reach me. Fortunately, however, the guards were probably too drowsy, and had been on the alert so long that they became inattentive. This was one of our most narrow escapes.

We were no more than safely across the road when a new and unseen obstacle, in the shape of a high fence, presented itself, over which we must climb before we could breathe free. We crawled carefully to the fence, and by great patience and much care, one at a time, managed to get over without attracting the attention of the guards. We felt as if we had accomplished quite an achievement, when at last we had escaped beyond the fence a few steps, and found ourselves in an open field, where we could push ahead noiselessly, and when, at last, we got away entirely out of hearing, we struck out on a full run. At the far side of the field we came to a small stream, in which we traveled some distance in the water, to take precaution against pursuit by dogs. Soon after, we struck a thick piece of woods on the slope of a hill-side, which we continued to ascend under the thick foliage for some time. But, at last, exhausted Nature asserted her full sway, and we were compelled to lie down and rest out of sheer inability to go further.

Up to this time, I think, neither of us had spoken, no more than if we had been dumb. As we threw ourselves on the ground, without breath or strength to go further for the time being, we began to realize the weak, helpless condition we were in. We had been so long shut up, without exercise and half starved, that to our surprise we found we had but little strength. It did not appear as if our limbs were strong enough to carry us five miles a day. When we looked forward to the long journey ahead of us, the hunger and fatigue, it looked a little discouraging. I think, however, a portion of this sense of physical prostration was caused by the sudden relaxation from the great mental strain and excitement, which had been upon us from the time of the jail-break and immediately preceding it. This, with the intense exertion in running, in our enfeebled condition, had well nigh completely unnerved us. We were wild, too, almost, with joy at our escape. I could scarcely restrain myself from shouting at the top of my voice:

"Glory to God on High! Free again! Liberty! Liberty! Praise God, from whom all blessings flow! D—n the rebels! D—n the rebellion! D—n the slave-cursed Confederacy!"

We felt alternately paroxysms of anger and contrition, and I should have felt a sense of great relief and joy if I could have sung some good old familiar hymn of other days in thanks for our almost miraculous deliverance.

Dear reader, if you have never been in prison as we had been, you can never feel the wild, almost childish joy that we miserable beings felt when we came to fully realize that we were once more free from our galling fetters; free from the prison gloom; free from the clutches of our inhuman captors, and that there was once more a prospect that we might again see our old flag, our old comrades, and the dear friends at home.

But we had but little time to rest, rejoice or feel thankful in. We had to address ourselves to a more serious task. Many contingencies yet stood between us and the goal of our hopes. Many armed enemies; many long, weary miles of travel; many rivers lay across our path, and many days of hunger and many sleepless nights, if we would succeed.

Before we escaped from the prison and after we had determined on an escape, I studied over the subject of routes very carefully. I had seen enough of night travel in the mountains about Chattanooga and along the Tennessee River, and well knew, that the probabilities of our being picked up, should we go in that direction, would be very much greater. I, therefore, decided in my own mind that, in case I had the good fortune to get away, I would strike out for the Gulf, and try to reach some of the vessels of the Federal blockading squadron. While this would be much the longest route, the distance, as near as I could calculate, being over three hundred miles, I thought there would be less vigilance and liability of pursuit in that direction. In this conjecture it turned out that I was correct. The country was entirely unknown to me, except a slight general idea I had of it from the school geographies. I only knew that the waters of the Chattahooche River, which flowed by west of Atlanta, entered the Gulf.

While we rested on the hill-side, I communicated, in a whisper, to Mark my views, and he readily agreed that he would go in any direction I thought best. Accordingly, we rose up and walked to an open place where we could see the stars, and soon determined our course, which was to be slightly south of west, and at once we set out as fast as we could travel. We spoke no words as we walked on, and went as noiselessly as possible, for we were watchfully on the look-out for scouting parties of cavalrymen that might be prowling about.

We soon came to the railroad track leading from Atlanta to Columbus and knew from this that our course was about right. Our march led us through some rough country and we were compelled to halt and rest quite frequently, so that when it began to grow light in the east we estimated that we were about eight miles from the prison. We sought out a secluded retreat for the day, and after getting each of us a stout stick, which would answer either as a weapon or a walking-stick, we lay down and slept until late in the afternoon. We woke up much rested, but were so lame and our feet were so sore that we could hardly take a step without excruciating pain. This was not to be wondered at, when our long confinement in prison and lack of exercise for weeks and months is considered. We were hungry, and the scanty morsel of corn-bread we had brought from the prison the previous, evening did not go far toward satisfying our sharp appetites. But it was all we had, and we ate it and were thankful, although we did not know where or when we would get our next rations.

I now saw a difficulty in this attempt to get away that we did not encounter in our first attempt to reach the Federal lines. Our clothes had become dirty and ragged, and we had a sort of jail-bird look, that it seemed to me would betray us if we were seen. I was brought to a realization of this fact as I looked at Wood, when we sat together in silence beneath the great tree where we had taken shelter, waiting for the friendly mantle of darkness to shield our movements. And I suppose my own appearance was no more prepossessing than his. The miserable garments he wore did not cover his nakedness. His face was begrimed with dirt almost set in the skin. He had become thin and emaciated with fever, and had a ravenous appetite; his eyes were sunken in his head and seemed to have the wild, unnatural glare of a madman, which at times almost made me shudder. The poor fellow's pitiable appearance, as he sat there despondently and longingly gazing down on the beautiful valley below was such as to appeal to a heart of stone. Yet I knew that it was unsafe for us to go to a house, and we agreed not to be seen by a human being if we could avoid it. I felt certain that if we should meet any one, our appearance would at once betray us. We were in a country where we could not expect to find a friend, unless, possibly, it might be the negroes, of whom, as a class, we knew but very little. We were so weak, and the mental strain and long-continued anxiety in which we had lived from day to day, had had the effect of making us, I may say foolishly suspicious and timid of everything. We were startled at every sudden noise, and crouched like sneaking wolves from the sight of man.

As I sat there and beheld the sun receding behind the hills in the west its long resplendent rays lighting up the beautiful valley below us, which seemed to smile in peace and plenty, I could not but think how much the Creator had done to make his creatures happy and contented beings, and how much they on their part had done to make themselves miserable. Why was I a miserable, forsaken, hungry outcast, shunning the sight of mv fellow beings in a civilized, (?) Christian (?) land, which the Creator had blessed with all the comforts necessary to the happiness of man? I could not help comparing our condition to that of Christian in "Bunyan's Pilgrim's Progress," who, on his way to the Celestial City, came into the Valley and Shadow of Death. We were not, it is true, like Christian, in a land of "deserts, and drouth," neither did we meet "hobgoblins, satyrs, and dragons," yet we were beset by equally disagreeable enemies, and our condition was one of "unutterable misery." We were not outlaws; we had done no crime, unless trying to serve our country was a crime. I sometimes wondered, like Job of old, why my afflictions were so great.

But repining does a fellow no good, and I have sometimes half questioned whether man's power of thought, reason, memory and reflection, really is so much of an advantage to him over the rest of the animal creation after all. If man had not these faculties he would not, at least, borrow trouble for the morrow, neither would he have the ingenuity and wickedness to persecute his fellow man, and turn that which an all-wise Creator made a paradise, into a place of torture and punishment.

While in the midst of these unpleasant thoughts, Mark broke the long silence by raising his head and saying:

"Alf, it is time for us to go."

Our journey that night took us through a corn-field, where we pulled a few ears of corn and chewed it as we went along. I remember it was very hard and made my jaws very tired, but it helped to quiet my gnawing hunger. It was much better than nothing. After a toilsome night's journey, guided by the stars, and over a very rough country, in which we entirely avoided roads, we again secreted ourselves as the streaks of gray began to appear in the east, and, after scraping up a pile of leaves, laid down for the day. When we awoke, late in the afternoon, we found that our feet were so bruised and sore, and that we were otherwise so lame, and withal so weak from hunger, that it taxed our endurance to the utmost to take a single step. We each took from our pockets an ear of corn, and after crunching and swallowing what we could, we put the rest in our clothes and hobbled off, making but very slow time for the first mile or so. It was in the month of October, and the nights were pretty cool, which, in our poorly-clad condition, compelled us to keep moving all the time to keep comfortably warm.

The next morning came and still we had not reached the river. Again we hid ourselves and slept through the day. When night came and we tried to walk, we found our feet in such a deplorable condition that it did not seem possible for us to go farther. They were blistered, galled and so feverish and swollen that it seemed as if they would burst with very pain at every step.

It began to be a serious question whether we would not have to give up traveling, and as we started, poor Mark crawled some distance on his hands and knees, and, looking back at me, said in an appealing tone, "Alf, what's a fellow's life but a curse to him when he has to drag it out in this way? I would rather be dead and done with it."

I encouraged him, telling him the worst was over and we would soon reach the river. I suppose we had shaped our course a little too far south and thus made the distance longer than it would otherwise have been. We struggled on for some time, sometimes crawling where the ground was stony, and stopping very often to temporarily quell the pain in our feet. I was a little ahead, and, as the breeze fanned my aching temples

I thought I heard to our right the lull of running water. I told Mark, and cheered him up. We forgot our tortures for the time being and scrambled on quite lively, and soon after had the satisfaction of standing on the banks of the Chattahooche.

De Soto did not feel more joy when he first discovered the Mississippi, the great Father of Waters, nor was the ecstacy of Balboa greater, when, from the cloud-capped summits of Darien, his eyes first beheld the vast expanse of water which he named the Pacific Ocean. Like that great discoverer, we waded out into the water, carrying neither naked sword nor the banner of our country like he, to take possession of our discovery in the name of our rulers, but to bathe our painful feet and cool our parched throats.

We both felt that we had gone as far as we could. Wood had been crawling on his hands and knees much of the time to spare his aching feet, while my condition was but little better. It did not seem to me that we could have gone a mile farther, but the discovery of the river inspired us with new hope. We sat down and chewed some more of our corn and rejoiced at our good fortune. We had left the Atlanta prison and gallows far behind. We were by waters that led to the great ocean, hundreds of miles away, where we might find friends and see the old flag once more.

I now felt like shouting for joy at the bright prospect before us. But our style of traveling did not admit of any noisy demonstration. We were rather imitating the peculiar traits of such night prowlers as the wolf and his sly congener, the fox. We made certain of the direction the river current ran, and started southward in high hopes, although the temptation to go northward to our friends was very strong. We now wanted a boat, and, not long after we started, fortune had another pleasant surprise in store for us, for we came upon a skiff safely moored, with lock and chain, to a tree. After carefully inspecting the surroundings, to see that no prying eyes were peering on us, we "loosened" the lock with a stone, and in a few minutes after were smoothly gliding down the current of the great river, and I doubt if two more joyful mortals ever navigated, a canoe than we two, with that stolen little craft.

What a. happy change! Our weary limbs and painful feet now had a rest, and yet we were gliding noiselessly on our journey. What wonderful teachers hardship and stern necessity are! Discontented mortals do not half appreciate the blessings they have until they have been pupils in the school of adversity. I felt as if this chilly night's ride, in a little stolen boat, in a strange river, whose shores were hidden by Plutonian shadows, was the best and most grateful that I ever had, or ever expected to enjoy.

We pulled off our old boots and bathed our lacerated feet in the water, and quenched the tormenting thirst caused by the indigestible hard corn, which was now our only nourishment. We kept our paddles pretty busy, as we wished to get as far away as possible from where we took the boat, before the dawn of day. When daylight began to appear, we paddled our craft into a bayou, safe from view, and secreted ourselves in a thicket for the day.

CHAPTER XIV.

The Pangs of Hunger—Visions of Feasting—We Must Have Food—Visit a Rebel Planter's House—Get a Good Meal—Hearing the News from Atlanta—How the Desperate Train-Thieves Broke Jail—A Tumble in the River—Mark Gets to "the End of the River"—A Mysterious Noise—Reckless Run Over a Mill-Dam—Narrow Escape amid Foaming, Dashing Waters and Rocky Gorges—Mark Falls in the River—A Toilsome Land Journey of Three Days and Nights—Passing Columbus—The Rebel Ram Chattahooche—Capture Another Boat—Soon Exchange It for a Better One—Pursued by Its Owners—How We Escape Them and Sweep Down the Broad River—Feeding on Corn and Pumpkin Seeds—Mosquitoes, Snakes and Alligators.

FOUR days and nights had now passed since we had eaten food, except the morsel of corn-bread we brought out of the prison, and the hard corn, which, with the copious use of river water, was beginning to cause great distress in our stomachs, which only added to the unpleasant pangs of hunger. We laid down to sleep the day away, but between our great hunger and the swarms of mosquitoes we could get but little rest. I could, while sleeping, see in my dreams, tables spread and groaning with loads of good things to eat; bread, meat, cheese, coffee, biscuit and butter were all within my reach, and were vanishing before my ravenous appetite, when in the midst of the great pleasures of this feast, I would suddenly waken to a sense of the reality of the case, and what a maddening disappointment I would feel. With this disturbed sort of rest we worried through the day, the demands of hunger and our stomachs getting the better of Nature's demand for rest, until at last we grew desperate, and at early twilight, in the evening, pulled out of the little bayou, determined on a raid of some sort, on a house for food, peaceable, if possible, forcible, if necessary.

At last, and before it grew too dark, we spied a house some distance from the river bank, which we thought, from appearances, we could capture with a plausible story, or by force, so we leisurely concealed our boat, and, in order to let it get quite dark, delayed our visit until a little later in the evening.

On approaching the house, we saw in its immediate vicinity quite a number of negro cabins, and in the yard surrounding the house, about twenty blood-hounds chained to the fence, indicating that these were the premises of an extensive planter. The only occupants of the house were an old man and woman. We apologized for disturbing them and told them we were soldiers who had been on furloughs returning to our regiments at Atlanta, and wished directions to the ferry (we had discovered a ferry as we came down); also, that we were hungry and wanted to get something to eat, provided they felt like feeding hungry soldiers without money, as we had had no pay for some time, and were both moneyless and in bad health, Mark's appearance proving this latter assertion. It was quite dark, however, and they could not see us very distinctly, but they evidently credited our story, for they told us to be seated and we would soon be made welcome to such food as they had.

They were a couple of quite intelligent, but unsophisticated old people, in comfortable circumstances, living as most Southerners did, away from any highway, and we gained their confidence so far as to feel ourselves assured from suspicion. I had been in Dixie so long that I had acquired, from the guards and citizens, their vernacular of speech quite perfectly; besides this, we had learned the names of officers and the number of different regiments, such as the Eighth Georgia cavalry, Fifth Tennessee infantry, etc., until we were able to tell quite a plausible story, if not too closely questioned.

We asked the old man if there was any late news; he said, "Nothing, except that the Yankee raiders had seized the Atlanta jailer, overpowered the guards, and a number of them escaped and had not yet been caught." We expressed, great surprise that such a piece of audacity could be made successful in Atlanta. The old man said "They were a desperate, dangerous lot of scoundrels, who ought to have been hung long ago." He said many of them stood up and fought the soldiers with clubs and brick, even after the guards had shot them through, and finally they jumped the high fence and run like deer.

He expressed his doubts about the South being able to beat back such a reckless band of robbers and freebooters as were swarming down from the Yankee country. He said all the worst class of low-down thieves and the scum of all the great cities of the North were hired to come down and take part against the South. We assured him that it would all come out right in the end, and the South would triumph; that one Southern man could whip five "Yanks" any day, and that there was no doubt of the final result.

In the meantime, we had devoured everthing the good woman had set before us on the table. We were ashamed, but our hunger was so much stronger than our sense of shame that we could not leave off, and if we had not been in a hurry, we would have waited for her to have prepared another meal for us. She said she regretted that she had not more cooked to set before us, but we told her she had been very kind and thanked them, at the same time bidding them good night, when we started off, as they supposed, for the ferry. A short time afterward we were in our boat pulling down stream with more vigorous energy than we had before. We kept up a steady stroke of the paddles for some hours, feeling that each stroke placed so much more distance between us and the prison.

While we were thus moving along with steady, cautious stroke, high in the hopes of the future, I suddenly, quicker than a flash, found myself lying flat on my back in the river. What on earth had happened I did not know, the accident had been so sudden. I thought of earthquakes, whales, sharks, torpedoes and many other things. Luckily, one of my feet caught on the side of the boat, and I drifted with it until Mark came to my assistance and pulled me out. The cause of my mishap had been a ferry-boat wire, which was stretched across the river, and hung just low enough to catch me fairly as I sat in the stern of the boat. It struck Mark, but he sat in the middle and fell into the bottom of the boat. We were going at a good speed, and the collision came so suddenly, that it is a wonder we did not fare worse. Fortunately, there were no guards at the ferry, so we had no cause to apprehend discovery or molestation. My greatest mishap was a thorough wetting, for the night was frosty and cold and caused me to chill.

This was followed in the after part of the night by a stupor that I could not shake off, and my continued efforts at the paddle had well nigh exhausted me. Mark could not manage the boat very well, as he had tried it a number of times. But I felt that I must have rest and sleep, and so gave the boat over into his hands, enjoining him to keep it in the current. I laid down in the bottom of the boat, and soon sank into a state of forgetfulness and sleep. I do not know how long I had slept, but, some time in the night, Mark aroused me, and told me we could go no further, as we had come "to the end of the river." It was some time before he could awaken me fully to consciousness, so that I could comprehend our situation.

At last I began to look around, to determine what Mark's "end of the river" meant. I soon discovered that he had run the boat away under a ledge of the mountain, and a dim light could only be seen in one direction. All else around us was impenetrable darkness. I took the paddle and worked the boat in the direction of the light, and in a little while we emerged from beneath this overhanging mountain ledge, and again reached the current of the river, down which the boat was soon rapidly gliding. Mark now discovered that the "end of the river" had not yet been reached, but he did not care to take charge of the boat again.

I have omitted to mention a matter, unimportant to

my story, although it shows how suspicious a fellow may become, when he imagines that every strange sound he hears may proceed from a lurking, pursuing enemy. Nearly the whole time, from the place where we began our boat journey, we seemed to be followed. At irregular intervals through the night, we would hear a noise in the water, always about the same distance behind us, which sounded precisely as if a large stone had suddenly fallen from a great height into the river. The noise never came much nearer, and never varied but little in distance, and always seemed to be just behind us. We were wholly unable to account for it, and we were thus somewhat vexed because we could not solve the mystery. Finally, one evening, as we started into the current from our hiding-place, and while it was yet quite light, we saw a good-sized animal swimming not far from us, and pretty soon it plunged under the water, making the identical mysterious noise we had heard. It followed, at least it seemed to be the same one, in our wake until we reached the rapids of the river above Columbus, after which we heard it no more. To this day I have not the remotest idea as to what kind of creature it was.

Shortly after this adventure, we perceived that we were not to have as smooth sailing all the way. The river began to grow rough, and the water ran over benches and ledges of rocks, and, in places, with great velocity, so much so that we narrowly escaped being "broken up," on several occasions during this night's journey. We passed over a number of places that we would not have dared to risk in daylight, when we could have seen the danger. It seemed to grow worse and worse as we went on, when daylight warned us that it was time to tie up and hide, which we did, and, the day being warm and pleasant, we had a comfortable rest—the best since our escape.

On the following night we came to a mill-dam, where the water, judging from the noise, poured over in great volume and force. We maneuvered around for some time above it, not knowing what to do, but finally discovered what appeared to be an apron, near the center of the dam, and decided to risk running it. Accordingly, we rowed up stream some distance to get under good headway, then turning the head of the boat down stream, we bent to our paddles with all our might. We came down with the velocity of an express-train. What we supposed might have been an apron, was nothing but a break in the dam, and over it we shot like an arrow, shutting our eyes and holding our breath. In an instant after, we landed (luckily right side up), away below, in the midst of the angry, foaming torrent, and plying our paddles right vigorously and keeping the bow of our boat down stream, we rode out safely, but then and there "swore off" on running mill-dams in the night.

We continued our journey, though the river was still rough and growing worse. We were constantly among rocks and foaming, headlong torrents of water, while steep rocky walls confined the stream to very narrow limits, and dark, shadowy mountain peaks loomed up in the back-ground, reminding us of the Tennessee about Chattanooga. We went on from bad to worse, until, at last, during the latter part of the night, we were incautiously drawn into a gorge, where, it seemed, that the destruction of our boat was inevitable. Such was the force and velocity of the water, that we lost all control of the boat, and, in one instant would be spinning around in a furious eddy until our heads were fairly dizzy, and in the next, we would be dashed against the rocks, until it seemed as if our boat would be splintered to pieces. We regarded our escape here as the narrowest we had made, and as quick as we could do so with safety, we landed on the rocks, and, with many regrets, abandoned our little craft, to begin a tedious, toilsome land journey of three days and nights, over rocky hills, bluffs and mountains along the river.

Just as we had landed the boat, Mark started to walk out, and, losing his balance, fell headlong into the river. With considerable difficulty I fished him out as soon as possible, and the early morning being quite cool, the poor fellow was chilled through and through, and it was with the greatest difficulty that I finally succeeded in getting him up into the mountains, and continued to exercise him by walking, so as to get up a good circulation of his blood. But he became so benumbed that I finally let him lie down, and gathered a lot of cedar boughs and piled them thickly over him, and then crawled in with him myself, and kept him as warm as possible. Here we slept and rested until late in the afternoon of that day, which became very warm under the bright rays of the sun.

This fall in the river was only one instance of Mark's exhausted condition during our journey down the Chattahooche. He would often stagger and reel about as a man who is stupefied with liquor, and at times he seemed to be almost blind, so that I was constantly on the watch, and oftentimes had to lead him by the hand and care for him as for a child.

Our progress was very slow, and, towards the last, extremely painful. The old bruises and blisters on our feet, which were not entirely healed, came back worse than ever, and much of the time we crept along on the rocks on our hands and knees, believing that if once we could get below this range of mountains, we would find navigable waters. We came in sight of several isolated cabins in these wild, rocky hills, where we managed to beg a little food on two different occasions, which helped us very much, for we were getting so weak that we could scarcely go five miles a day. The suffering we endured on our last night's travel, I cannot describe. It seemed as if we must give up, and die were we were. But at last, when daylight came, to our great delight, we saw the spires and smoke stacks of a town in the distance. We knew this to be Columbus, Georgia, and that when we got below it, the river was navigable clear to the Gulf.

We now deemed it prudent to hide ourselves for the day, which we had not done in the mountains, and wait for the friendly cloak of darkness. When night came, we made a long, careful detour, away out around the suburbs of the town, and at last had the satisfaction of again reaching the river bank, below the town, where we found good shelter among the dense grapevines and drift-wood. By this time it was nearly morning again, and, like beasts of prey, we betook ourselves to a safe hiding-place.

During all the time we had been in the vicinity of

the town, we had heard a constant, clattering sound, as of a hundred workmen with hammers. This noise came from near the river, where there appeared also to be a great light. When daylight came the noise still continued, and we were near enough so that we could see that it was caused by a large number of workmen, engaged on a vessel, which they were covering with iron. The boat appeared to be very large and of great strength, and evidently was intended for a warlike purpose. On closer inspection, the following night, I found that she was a powerfully-built gunboat, which they were evidently in great haste to complete, as the hammers of the workmen never ceased on her, night or day, nor for a single moment.

This gunboat was none other than the rebel ram Chattahooche, a formidable iron monster, built as an engine of destruction for the blockading fleet in Appalachicola Bay. The first knowledge the Navy Department had of her was through Wood and myself. The ram, on her first downward trip, blew up, near the mouth of Flint River, and never reached the Gulf.

Our great anxiety now was to secure a boat. Wood was so lame he could not walk, and I was not much better. This delayed us here two days and nights. During the nights, I was prowling about, up and down, trying to discover some sort of a craft that would float. In my reconnoitering about the gun-boat, I had discovered an old skiff chained to a stump, quite near and in plain sight of the workmen, to some of whom, no doubt, it belonged. I secured a stout stick for a lever, and crept to the stump to which the boat was chained, when, watching my opportunity, I got a pry in such a manner as to break the lock on the chain. The lights shone so brightly that I could plainly see the men's eyes, and I very much feared they would notice me. However, I worked off with the boat carefully, and half an hour after, I had Mark aboard and we were pulling rapidly down stream. We found our prize to be a leaky old concern, and one of us was constantly busy keeping her bailed out.

After we had drifted down some miles, we spied three boats tied to the shore on the Alabama side of the river, and as we had been giving our attention entirely to the Georgians all along, we concluded to trade boats on that side of the river, provided we could secure a better boat. Just as we had got loosened the one we selected, three men with a pack of dogs were coming down the hill toward us, and the head man, evidently the owner, began hallooing to us and calling us slanderous names, such as thieves and the like. We did not stop to bandy words with the fellows, but speedily shoved all the boats into the river, and took a course up the river, as though we were going toward Columbus. They rent the air with curses upon our heads. In the course of fifteen or twenty minutes, they had secured the boats we shoved into the stream, and with the lights they carried, we could distinctly see that they were bent on pursuing us. We took a wide circuit, and then headed downward under cover of the willows, behind several small islands near the Georgia shore, and came out in the main stream far below the islands, while we had the satisfaction of seeing the lights of our pursuers disappearing up the river, and prowling about the upper end of the islands, which we were now leaving far behind us. We soon lost sight of them, and the strong presumption is that they never succeeded in finding their boat.

We increased our speed to the utmost, and kept under the shadows of the wooded shores as much as possible, congratulating each other on our lucky boat trade. With a good boat and an open river we felt now that our chances of escape were exceedingly good, and our spirits were buoyant and hopes high, although our stomachs were craving food. We were on the verge of starvation all the time, for we had eaten food only three times, not counting the corn and morsel of bread, since we started, although we had been traveling every night, and, in the mountains, both day and night.

When I look back and think of those long, painful, hungry nights and days, I wonder how it was possible that we kept up. I do not think I could withstand the same deprivation again, although a man does not know what he can endure until he tries it. I believe a human being can endure greater hardships and longer-continued suffering than any other animal. Hunger was now our main dread. We felt that our paddles and the stiff current of the river were good for fifty miles each night, provided we could keep from starving. To be sure, we were used to fasting; indeed, for months not a day had passed that we had not felt the pinching distress of an unsatisfied longing for food. But on we swept, hour after hour, down the broad river, happy in the thought that we were fast placing scores of miles between us and the hated prison. The rest given our feet had much allayed the pain we had suffered, and when morning came and we had secreted ourselves for the day, we slept well, but awoke in the afternoon ravenously desperate for want of something to eat.

We went out, and, reconnoitering a little, discovered a corn-field. Making sure that there was no one about, we stole into the field and found plenty of corn and pumpkins. The hard corn and river water did not go well together, and proved to be an unpleasant diet to us, so we broke up the pumpkins, ate freely of the seed, and filled our pockets with more for lunch, each of us taking also a few ears of corn. By the time we got back, it was nearly dark, and we pulled out. The pumpkin-seed diet, poor as it was, helped us wonderfully, and we made a big night's journey, passing a steamboat upward bound, which we dodged by pulling under the shadows of the timber and low-hanging bushes.

Thus we progressed, traveling by boat at night, and laying by in the daytime. If any reader of this story has ever made a trip on the lower end of the Chattahooche River, I think he or she will agree with me when I say that the river scenery is peculiarly monotonous, and causes a sense of loneliness. It is a vast water-path through dense forests of cypress and other swamp-growing timber. On either side, to the right and left, were endless swamps covered with water, and the river channel was only observable by its being free from logs and gigantic trees. Great festoons of gray and sombre moss hung suspended from even the topmost limbs of these trees, reaching clear down to the water, and floated and swung to the music of the sighing winds. Perhaps it was the circumstances in our case that made us feel so, but I remember it as a dismal, lonesome journey. Sometimes we would not see a sign of civilization for forty-eight hours at a stretch.

Besides the torments of hunger, our nights were made almost unendurable by the swarms of blood-thirsty mosquitoes, which came upon us in clouds. I did think that I had learned considerable about mosquitoes in my boyhood days, in the Black Swamp of Northwestern Ohio, but for numbers, vocal powers and ferocity, I will "trot" the Chattahooche swamp fellows out against any others I have ever "met up with.' The ragged clothing, which yet clung to our backs, did not much more than half cover us; especially was this the case with Wood, who was, I may truthfully say, half naked, and was thus doubly annoyed by the omnipresent "skeeters." And my own condition was but little better. To protect ourselves from the pests, we thatched our bodies all over with great skeins of moss, and two more comical-looking beings than we were, thus rigged out, it would be hard to find, but it baffled the bills of our tormentors.

We had two other annoyances—moccasin snakes and alligators. The latter, with which the water swarmed as we went further toward the Gulf, were a terror to me. They were a ferocious, hungry, dangerous-looking beast at best. We knew but little of their habits. The largest water inhabitant I had ever seen was a Maumee River catfish, and the most dangerous, a Black-Swamp massasauger. Night or day, these "gators," as the Southern negroes call them, like the mosquitoes, were always within sight and hearing. Sometimes, during the day, in order to keep out of the water, we would take shelter in a pile of drift-wood. When we would wake up, after a short nap, every old log and hommock about us would be covered with "gators." They would lay listlessly and lazily, with eyes almost shut, looking hungrily and quizzically out of one corner of their wicked peepers, as if waiting for us to leave, or for a chance to nab one of us by the leg or arm and run. Mark grew superstitious of these creatures. He said he had read of wolves following a famished buffalo in the same manner, and that sharks would hover around a ship from which a corpse was to be cast overboard, and that, too, even days before death had occurred or was even suspected by the sailors. But the "gators" were cowardly fellows, and, on the least demonstration on our part, would scramble into the water. Still, we feared they might steal upon and lay hold of us with their powerful jaws while we were asleep. We had learned that they were not apt to attack, except when the object of their voracious appetites lay quiet, but, when once they did lay hold, that they were hard to beat off. They will drag their victim, be it man or beast, instantly under the water, where the struggle soon ends.

CHAPTER XV.

Again Go After a Meal—In Our Absence Our Boat is Stolen—Our Feelings of Despair—A Night of Gloom—Dangerous Method of Securing Another Boat—Complete Success, and We Go on Our Way Rejoicing—A Feast on Raw Cat-fish and Corn—Mark Wood's Famished, Frenzied Condition—Nearing the Gulf—Appalachicola—Visit a House to Light My Pipe and Get Information—A Royal Feast on Cooked Fish and Roasted Sweet Potatoes—Going Down the Bay—Looking for the Blockading Fleet—Going through an Oyster Bed—The Federal Fleet in the Distance—Thrilling, Rapturous Sight—We See the Old Flag Once More.

"Hail! starry emblem of the free!"

WE were now journeying in a place where our means of getting food were poor indeed, for there was no food. After enduring hunger as long as we possibly could, we were finally forced a second time, since leaving Columbus, to go in search of something to eat. This, I think, was about five or ten miles above Chattahooche landing. It is not necessary to relate the particulars of our search for a human habitation and the story of deception we told. It was a little before dark, when we struck out on foot, so weak, hungry and faint that we could not walk many steps without resting, in search of something or anything we could devour. We were successful, or partially so, at least, and came back safely, much strengthened, as well as elated over our good luck, when, to our great dismay and chagrin, we found that our boat had been stolen during our absence.

It was evident some one had seen us land and watched until we left, and then taken the boat. I cannot describe our feelings. We scarcely knew what to do. The night was very dark, and it rained incessantly. We waded about in the water, tall grass and cane, and after a while found a little mound or hommock, which projected above the water, and on which we perched ourselves for the night. Such a dismal, long, rainy night as it was, too! It did seem as if the mosquitoes would carry us away piecemeal towards morning, when the rain had ceased. Had it not been for the food we had eaten, I believe we would have given up in despair. When morning came, we waded up and down in the cane and grass all forenoon, and about the only discovery we made, was that another river came in just below us and we could not go further without a boat.

During the afternoon I descried something on the far side of the river that looked like a boat partly sunk in the water, one end only of which was out. The next trouble was to get to it, as the river was about three-quarters of a mile wide, as near as we could judge. We found an old piece of plank, which we lashed on three flat rails with a grape-vine, and with a piece of narrow stave for a paddle and to fight off "gators," I twined my legs firmly around the center of the frail craft, while Mark pushed it off into the stream and stood at the edge of the grass watching me. The raft sunk down until the water came about my waist, but I stuck to it, and after about an hour's hard work, I effected a landing on the far side, and, not long after, found myself rewarded in the possession of a much better boat than the one we had lost the night before. I was not long in bailing out the water and rowing her back to where Mark was, whose gratitute found expression in tears and hearty hand-shaking, as he crept into the boat with me.

We now plied our paddles energetically for a while, until we felt sure we had passed out of reach of the owners of the boat, when we put into the cane and secreted ourselves until night. After this mishap in losing our boat, we resolved that we would not both leave again while our journey lasted, starve or no starve. During the following day, while we were laid up waiting for night and fighting mosquitoes, I went out, skulking about to see what I could see, and in passing through an old field found some fish-hooks and lines in an old vacant cabin. I appropriated them, and we found them a godsend to us, for they proved the means of keeping us from actual starvation.

The country, from the point where we then were, on both sides of the river, nearly to the gulf, seemed to be but one endless expanse of swamp, with scarcely a human inhabitant, or, indeed, any spot or place where a human could make a permanent home. It was the most forsaken, desolate country of all we had seen. We could find nothing, not even corn, to subsist on now; but we had quite a fair supply tied in bark and dragging after us in the water, that it might soak soft and be a little more palatable. The effects of this raw corn on us had been very bad. Our stomachs had become feverish, and it caused sharp pain and some ailment akin to cholera-morbus.

We must have had a touch of scurvy, for our mouths and gums had become feverish, and our teeth were loose, and would bleed constantly when we attempted to chew the corn. This was the condition we were in when, providentially, we became possessed of the fish-hooks and lines.

And now for a feast on raw cat-fish, of which we caught a plentiful supply as we journeyed on in the night. I have previously neglected to mention that I had with me an old one-bladed knife without any back, which was our only weapon, defensive or offensive. This old knife I had secreted when we were in the Atlanta prison, and had kept it with me as a precious treasure during all our wanderings. With this knife and our fingers, we managed to skin and dress the fish, which we ate raw with our soaked corn. Matches, we had none, nor had we been able to get any, and so we had no fire. I could eat only a mouthful or two of the raw fish at a time. My stomach was weak and feverish, and rebelled against the flesh. Still it tasted palatable.

Mark, poor, hungry fellow, tore it from the bones in great mouthfuls, like a ravenous wolf, until I would beg of him to desist, fearing the results. He would set and crunch the bloody flesh, and look at me with a wild, strange stare, and never speak a word. His eyes were sunken away in his head, almost out of sight, and as he would seize a fresh piece, the pupils of his eyes would dilate with the gloating, ferocious expression of a panther or other carniverous wild beast. I had frequently heard of men losing their reason and going mad from the effects of protracted hunger, and I sometimes shuddered as I looked at its telling effects on poor Mark's wasted frame, and the unnatural glare of his eyes. He would mutter and groan in his sleep, and sometimes scream out as if pierced by a knife, when he would suddenly start up and call my name. Toward the last of our journey his condition was, much of the time, a cause of great anxiety to me. Still, after we began to eat the fish, he seemed much better, and I only feared the unnatural quantities of the raw flesh he ate would kill him.

The reader who enjoys three regular meals each day, can better understand our condition when I state that from the time we left the mountains above Columbus, to the time of which I am now speaking, where we found the fishing-tackle, a period of nearly two weeks, we had eaten but four meals, aside from the stuff we had picked up, such as raw pumpkins, corn, roots and pumpkin-seed, all of which we obtained in very limited quantities.

We were now nearing the bay, as was plain to be seen, for on each succeeding morning the river had grown wider. Finally we became well satisfied that we were nearing a large town, which afterwards proved to be Appalachicola, and this made us anxious to learn something of the state of affairs below--whether there were rebel picket-boats, or obstructions, such as torpedo-boats and the like.

About this time we discovered a cabin some distance from the shore, and, to have a plausible excuse, I took an old pipe Mark had, and filled it with a few crumbs of tobacco, which I fished from my old coat-linings, and then taking a piece of rotten wood, which would retain fire, I left Mark with the boat and walked over to the house to get a light for my pipe. The occupants of the cabin proved to be an old Scotchman and his wife. He was very inquisitive, and asked more questions than I cared to answer. But I managed to evade suspicion, and at the same time gained considerable information. I learned that we were about five miles above Appalachicola, and that the Federal blockading squadron was stationed at the mouth of the bay, eighteen miles below the city. I hurried back to the boat, and found Mark rejoicing over a little armful of sweet-potatoes he had stolen from a negro's canoe, which he had discovered in my absence.

We got into the boat and at once paddled to the other side of the bay or river, where we entered into an inlet or creek, up which we ran for some distance, when we came to a dense cane-brake. Here we secreted ourselves and built a little fire, roasted fish and potatoes, parched corn, and dined in right royal style, although we felt the need of a little salt. Two hungry wolves never ate more ravenously than we did, although we were obliged to restrain ourselves, and leave off while yet hungry. It was with the utmost difficulty that I absolutely forced Mark to quit. After eating enough for four men, as I thought, he still begged for more. I finally induced him to go to sleep, and stored away some of the cooked fish and sweet potatoes for the next day.

The information we had gained was invaluable to us, although I felt I had obtained it at some risk. When night came on, we pulled out and passed down on the opposite side of the bay from the city, slowly and cautiously.

We had moss in the bottom, on the sides and in the seats of our boat for our comfort. As soon as we had gone well past the city, whose bright lights we could plainly see, we crossed the bay to the city side below the city, in the hope of finding a more sea-worthy boat. We were unable to find any other boat, however, and pulled on down the bay as fast as we could. While going down the bay that evening, we ran along in the midst of a large school of huge fish of some description, from which we apprehended danger every instant. These monsters would swim along on all sides of us, with great fins sticking more than a foot out of the water, and extended like a great fan. They would frequently whisk their fish-shaped tails above the water, which seemed to be as much as three to four feet across from tip to tip. One of these fish could easily have wrecked our boat with its huge body. I have never been able to learn to what class these finny monsters belonged. We hoped to reach the blockading fleet before daylight, but the night grew cloudy and we were unable to tell what course we were running, as the bay grew wider and wider as we went out. We decided the best thing we could do was to pull for land, which we reached after midnight, pretty well exhausted with our hard work at the paddles. We tied up our boat and went to a thicket near by and slept soundly.

When we awoke in the morning, we were cheered by the beautiful surroundings—all just as nature had fashioned them, for the habitation or handiwork of man was nowhere to be seen. Our couch had been a bed of prickly grass, that caused a stinging, itching sensation all over our bodies. We had slept in a wild orange grove. The shore was lined with the lemon, the orange, and the palm tree, besides many other varieties of which I knew nothing. The leaves of the palm were so large that we could lie down and completely cover ourselves with a single leaf. These beautiful groves and shores had no charms for us in the present case, however. We were looking for the Federal blockading fleet.

We made a hasty breakfast on our fish and potatoes left from the night previous, and started for our boat; but imagine our surprise when we found it distant at least two hundred yards from the water. Mark, who had lived in the old country, explained to me that this was the effect of the ocean tide, which had gone out since we landed, and would not come in again until that night. There was no safe course left us but to drag our boat to the water, which we did, after tugging at it for about an hour.

When we were again on the water we could see the spires and high buildings of the city we had passed, but no sight of ships could we see. We took our course as well as we could, and pulled for the open sea. A little boat, which seemed to be a fishing smack, under full sail, passed away to the leeward of us, coming out from the city, and caused us no little concern, but she passed off and either did not notice us or care to inquire who we were. We plied our paddles industriously until about the middle of the afternoon, when we spied an island away in the distance. We had been out of sight of land for some time, and the view of the island cheered us up a little, for we knew if a rough sea came on that our little boat was liable to get swamped. This island was much further away than we had supposed. As we neared it we were in some doubt as to whether we should pass to the right or left of it, when our decision was made by the discovery to the left and away in the distance, of something that had the appearance of dead trees.

In the same direction, and right in our course, was something that appeared like a bar or gravel bank. We supposed the old trees stood on another low island or bar beyond. But, as we neared this bar, that which at first seemed to be dead trees, began to take the shape of ship-masts, and we imagined that we could see something that looked like the dark outlines of black smoke-stacks in the blue, hazy distance. This made us quite nervous, and we pulled away at the paddles with renewed vigor and strength. Before we were scarcely conscious of it, we were close upon the bar, and began to be puzzled how we should get by or around it, for it was longer than it appeared to be when first seen. Presently we discovered a narrow, shallow channel through it, and we were not long in getting our boat through. As we were going through, Mark gathered in a lot of rough, muddy-looking lumps, which I supposed were boulders, and soon called for my old broken-backed knife, after which I saw him open one of the muddy chunks and eat something from it. Says I:

"Mark! you starving Yank! what in thunder are you at now."

"Taste this," says he, as he opened another muddy chunk, and I lapped up from the dirty shell the sweetest oyster I had ever tasted.

We were in the midst of a great oyster bed, the like of which I had never before seen. I had never, in fact, seen an oyster in the shell before. Mark gathered up as many as he could as the boat passed along, and when we reached the still water, we made quite a little feast on them as we paddled on. I think I never tasted anything so delicious. We were still very hungry, and the moist, rich, salty flavor of the oysters seemed to suit our weak, famished stomachs to a nicety.

But our little feast was soon cut short by the certain discovery that the dead trees were nothing less than the masts of vessels. We could now plainly see the yards, cross-trees and great smoke-stacks. We dropped the oysters in the bottom of the boat, and, though quite exhausted, the sight of the vessels so renewed our strength that we made the little boat scud over the still water at a lively rate. Soon we could see the long, graceful streamers waving from the peaks of the masts, and the outlines of the dark, sombre-looking hulls of the ships.

We were now nearing the ships very fast, and were a little anxious to see their colors, as we had become so suspicious of everybody and everything that we half feared running into the clutches of our enemies. But we were not long in suspense, for suddenly a little breeze sprang up, and I shall never, no, never, forget my joy on seeing the old flag, the glorious old stars and stripes, as they unfolded to the ocean breeze and seemed to extend their beneficent protection over us, after nearly eight months of terrible bondage. We could see the field of blue, studded with its golden stars, and the stripes of white and red! Yes, it was our flag, old

E Pluribus Unum! We threw down our paddles in the boat and stood up and yelled and screamed and cried like a couple of foolish boys lost in the woods. We could not restrain ourselves. Mark wanted to jump overboard and swim to the ships, although we were yet, perhaps, nearly a mile away—at least, too far to swim in his condition. After we recovered our senses a little, we picked up the paddles and began rowing again, directing our course toward the largest vessel.

It seems now like a dream to me—that joyful day—the most joyful, I was about to say, of my life. I believe there were three vessels in sight. In steering for the largest one, although it was the most distant, we had to pass some distance in front of the bow of a smaller ship or boat. We were now getting so close that we could plainly see the officers and men on the decks, in their neat, blue uniforms. We could see the port-holes in the sides of the ships, and the black muzzles of the cannon projecting out. This gave us much assurance, and we said to ourselves:

"Good bye, rebs! We are out of your clutches at last!"

CHAPTER XVI.

Hailed by the Commander of the Blockading Fleet—A Gruff Reception—Explanation of Our Appearance—Changed Demeanor of the Commander—Our Cadaverous Condition—Our Unbounded Joy—Rage of the Old Sea Veteran, Commander J. F. Crossman—A Kind and Noble Man—The Substantial Welcome Given Us—We Start for Key West—Dreams of the Terrible Past—Yellow Jack Catches Me—Key West —The "Conchs" —A Marked Contrast.

WE were rowing our insignificant-looking little boat right along, just as though we intended to capture the biggest vessel in the fleet, when a gruff voice from the ship, whose bow we were passing, commanded us to "Come to, there!" At the same time we saw a grim-looking old sea-dog, in nice uniform, leaning over the rail, motioning us in with his hand. We turned the bow of our little boat toward him, and, when we came within better speaking distance, he interrogated us, in stentorian voice, about as follows:

"Who in h—l are you, and what are you paddling under my guns in this manner for?"

We were half terrified by the old fellow's angry, stern manner, and did not know but we had at last fallen into the hands of a rebel cruiser under false colors. We did not know what to say to this unexpected, angry interrogation. We paddled on very slowly, while the sailors and officers began to gather in little squads and look at us with mingled curiosity and merriment.

Presently, the officer hailed us again, with about the same questions. I now stood up in our boat, and answered, that we were two men trying to get back to God's country, among friends. I was now quite uneasy and suspicious of the situation, and kept my eyes on the officer, for I perceived he was the commander. I shall never forget his stern, but puzzled look, as we came up under the bow of his vessel. We had been so overjoyed and excited, that we had forgotten to pull the old moss, which covered our nakedness and protected us from the sun, from our backs, and we must have looked like scare-crows or swamp-dragons. I cannot speak so well of my own appearance then, but can see Mark Wood, just as he was on that joyful day, and a more comical, forlorn, starved-looking being cannot well be imagined.

In our boat were a few cat-fish partly skinned, some oysters in the shell, some ears of scorched corn, a lot of moss and our old boots, for our feet were yet sore and we went bare-footed when in the boat.

After scrutinizing us in silence for some little time as we drifted up closer and closer, he again demanded of us some account of our strange conduct and appearance. I told him we were enlisted Federal soldiers, and belonged to the command of General O. M. Mitchell, in Tennessee, to which he growled something about our being a "d—d long ways from camp." I then explained to him briefly that we were fugitives, and the causes that led to it; that we were nearly famished with hunger, and that after skulking through mountains and river by night, we had at last sought protection under the old flag and the guns of his ship.

I could see that his manner toward us had changed. He plainly saw the indications of our distress. He said he had heard of the raiding expedition we spoke of, and commanded us to row up to the ladder and come up the ship's side. We did so, and Wood went up the steps first. The poor fellow's agitation and joy were so great, and he was so weak that he could scarcely raise his feet from step to step on the ladder, or stairs. The commander seeing his weak, faltering condition, leaned over the rail, as Wood came up, and, reaching out, took hold to assist him, and, as he did so, the rotten bit of old moss, which covered Mark's shoulders and back, all pulled off and exposed his emaciated, bony skeleton, which, in truth, was nothing but skin and bones. The well-fed, sleek-looking sailors seemed to look on in horror, but not more so than the generous-hearted commander, who was moved almost to tears, as he was reaching over to help me as I came to the top of the step-ladder. They stared at us in silent wonderment, while the sailors looked down into our little boat with comical curiosity.

No pen can tell my feelings when I fully realized that I was under the dear old flag and among friends, for such we found them. Mark was so overcome that he could scarcely speak, and so weak that he could hardly stand. It was with much effort that I was able to choke down my feelings, so that I could answer the few questions asked me. Pretty soon the old commander's anger got the better of him, and he raved and swore as he paced up and down, and stamped the deck until the air seemed fairly blue with brimstone. I think if he could have gotten hold of old Jefferson Davis, or some other first-class rebel, about that time, he would have hung him, and then tried him afterwards.

The vessel we had boarded was the United States gun-boat *Somerset,* of the Gulf blockading squadron, and the officer in command, who had taken us up, was Lieutenant-Commander J. F. Crossman. Peace to his ashes. It was with unfeigned sorrow that I learned, since I began writing these sketches, of his death, by accident, in the year 1872. A nobler, more kind-hearted and more sympathetic man for those in distress, never wore the United States uniform. He ordered us each a new suit of clothes, and gave orders to his cook to get dinner for us. He conducted us to the cabin, dirty and ragged as we were, and gave us each a few swallows of brandy, after which, he sent us aft with the sailors, to wash up, which we did with soap, the first time we had used the article since we had left our comrades at Shelbyville, nearly eight months before. We then rigged ourselves out in sailor's clothes, after which we were invited to the commander's cabin, where we took dinner with him.

We were so hungry that we were ashamed to even attempt to satisfy our appetites, although we were made welcome to everything he had. It seemed to me as though I could not get filled up. The commander talked freely with us, and cordially invited us to stay with him until we were recruited up, but we told him we would like to get back as soon as possible, or to some part of the Federal lines where we could report, and, if possible, save our comrades in the Atlanta prison, if the poor fellows were not already executed. He told us he would be pleased to have us stay until we were recruited from our starved condition, and that we would be made welcome on his vessel, but, that if we insisted on going right on he would signal a cruiser then lying not far away, to await further orders, which he did. This was the large looking vessel we had been steering for when hailed by Commander Crossman, and which was just ready to set sail for Key West.

After dinner, he interviewed us further, and again fell into a swearing frenzy. I thought he was the maddest, most furious swearer I had ever heard or seen. He wrote and forwarded dispatches to the Navy, and, I think, to the War Department, for my understanding of the case, at the time, was, and is still, that Secretary Stanton at once took the matter in hand, and notified the Confederate authorities at Richmond, that any further executions of the members of the Mitchell party would be met with prompt retaliation. My reason for thinking so will appear further on in my story. The commander also gave us letters to the commandants at the naval station at Key West and other points in our route. He furnished us with everything he could think of to make us comfortable, even to a supply of tobacco, and with a hearty farewell hand-shake and wishes for better fortune in the future and a safe voyage, the noble old man sent us off in a boat to the cruiser, on whose great dark hull was lettered her name, *Stars and Stripes*. We cast many a grateful look back at Commander Crossman, as he leaned over the rail looking after us, and to the last of my life shall I associate his name and that of his boat, the *Somerset*, with that eventful day of my existence, when Providence delivered me up from a miserable bondage, and almost a lingering death, into the hands of so kind and generous a friend.

Soon after we came on board the *Stars and Stripes*, she took up her anchor and was under way for Key West, and, soon after, we were out of sight of a land, where so many sorrows came upon us, and for which we had but few pleasant memories. I crept upon the upper deck, and for the first time in my life, gazed out upon the majestic ocean. I was almost dazed in grateful admiration at my changed condition and the sublime strange surroundings. Tears would come unbidden in my eyes, and it all seemed a dream. At times I would involuntarily start up, as if to flee from the sight of some one. It seemed like a beautiful dream, too good to be true. Even while I was awake, I almost doubted the reality of my situation. When I attempted to sleep I would be haunted with unpleasant visions of the terrible past. I could see Andrews, and hear his clanking chains. I could see our poor comrades who were executed, and the brutal officers and guards who dragged them away from us. My slumbers were haunted with visions of the old Atlanta jail, and the prison guards, and I could hear them shout, "Halt! halt!" as plain as when I ran from them on the day of my escape, and sometimes in my sleeping efforts at running, I would wake to find myself in a lively state of perspiration. This mental strain had been on me so long, and I was, physically, so reduced, that I found it next to impossible to shake off the spell. My brain was feverish, and as the strain began to relax, I began to feel drowsy, my appetite ceased, and before the third day of the voyage, my vitality, energy and strength seemed almost entirely gone. I felt the insidious but sure clutches of fever seizing upon me. My almost iron constitution had been overtaxed, and was gradually being overcome by disease, and on the fourth day, when we arrived at Key West, I knew or cared but little what became of me.

The surgeons pronounced my ailment yellow fever. I was taken to a physician's house, where I did not want for care and medical attendance. The place was garrisoned by a New York regiment, the Sixty-Ninth, perhaps, the officers and men of which treated us with great kindness and consideration.

After the fever had run its course and under the good treatment I was receiving, my condition improved very rapidly. As soon as the disease had entirely left me, my ravenous appetite began to return, and I hungered constantly, although my stomach was so weak that I dare eat only the least morsel at a time, and that of the very lightest kind of food. I did not know but I was to starve in the midst of friends and abundance. I attributed this weak, irritated condition of my stomach to the eating of raw, hard corn, although the doctor said it came about from a combination of causes. During my sickness, Mark had prevailed upon the commandant at Key West to urgently renew our request to the Secretary of War, at Washington, to take immediate steps to save the lives, if they yet lived, of those of our comrades who had not been so fortunate as to make their escape.

As soon as I got strong enough, I spent some time,

while we were waiting for a vessel to sail, in looking about this wonderful sea-girt reef. Key West is one of the extreme westerly islands of the group known as the Pine Islands. It is about sixty miles from the southern point of Florida, and is less than one hundred miles from the coast of Cuba. The island is about five miles long, and, I judge, a couple of miles wide, and the land or sand and rocks do not appear to be more than ten feet above the ocean level. The rock is coral and the island, so far as soil is concerned, presents a miserable, poor, starved appearance. There is a little salt lake or pond of three or four hundred acres on the island, and a couple of light-houses. Key West City—that is, the town of Key West, which takes its name from the island on which it is built—is a place, or was at the time of my visit, of two or three thousand inhabitants, the greater portion of whom are a mongrel set of human beings, from the Bahama islands, called "Conchs." They are not a desirable people to live among, according to my notions of society, although I would prefer them to Southern Confederacy rebels, two to one. These Conchs are a hardy, dare-devil sort of people, who seem as much at home in the water as a muskrat or alligator. Their business in life is fishing and wrecking, and it was told me by white men, that these islanders can dive to the bottom of the ocean, if it is not over fifty feet deep.

These Florida Key waters are very dangerous, and many an unfortunate vessel goes to the bottom or to pieces in this part of the Gulf every year, and these people sometimes do both a profitable and humane business in saving the crews of vessels and the cargoes. The air here, even in winter, is soft and balmy, and is said to be healthy, although it was too warm to suit me. The United States has a strongly fortified post, called Fort Taylor, on the island, which is so situated that it is capable of making a strong defense if assailed by ships of war. About sixty miles away, is another similar island, named Tortugas, where there is also a United States fort, and where a number of rebel prisoners were serving out sentences of various crimes.

These reefs and islands, and the ocean scenery and views, were all new and strange to me, and I was strongly impressed, not only with the wonders of Nature here, but the vastness of our country and its varied resources, products and climate. Here were a people who lived almost without need of clothing or houses, and on the products of the ocean, while I, who came from a part of the same great land and government, under the same flag, lived where warm clothes, houses and much other care was necessary for personal comfort, and entirely from the products grown from the earth, produced by a careful, assiduous round of labor from one season to another. Yet I would not swap an Ohio home, with its comfortable houses, orchards, gardens and privileges of schools, churches and society, with its regular habits and vital life and energy, for the luxurious, lazy, listless, useless lives, lived by people without necessities, without energy and without effort, in the tropical and semi-tropical climates, and especially with the wandering, vagabond Conchs. When a man can get a living with his fish-hook and line, and requires no greater shelter than a shade tree, and his greatest concern and comfort is his pipe and tobacco, there is not much to be expected from him.

CHAPTER XVII.

Port Royal—Death of General O. M. Mitchell—Memories of the Past—A Noble and Brave Commander—Characteristics of Successful Generalship—General Mitchell's Confidence in the Success of the Enterprise—Tribute Due to Our Beloved General—Steaming to New York with the Body of General Mitchell—Our Cordial Reception—Feted Everywhere—Arrival at Washington—Caught without a Pass and Imprisoned —A Note to the President—Immediate Release—Introduced to President Lincoln—His Kind Reception—An Interesting Interview — The President's Promise.

THE regiment that was doing garrison duty on the island received orders to go to Port Royal, while we were with them, and we took passage to that place on the same boat. On our arrival we learned a piece of news that caused us much sorrow. Only a short time before, our old division commander, General Ormsby M. Mitchell, had breathed, his last in that place, where he had been placed in command but a little while before the yellow fever seized upon him and carried him off.

What a privilege it would have been to us to have reached the place and seen him before his death. I recall his almost prophetic words on that memorable evening, far away in Tennessee, as beneath the canopy of a little clump of trees, we silently gathered about him to hear his last instructions to us, and at the conclusion of which he shook hands with each man and said, as the tears seemed to start from his eyes, "Boys, I fear I shall never see you again." Nor did he ever see one of the little band again, and I believe he died in the thought that our lives had all been sacrificed. And if he did die, so believing, it was a cause of pain and sorrow to him, for his was a noble, humane and sensitive nature, a soul of honor—too merciful to wield the bloody sword of a Marlborough or Blucher in war's carnage, and too honorable to sacrifice the humblest private in his army, to gratify ambition, or to exalt his own fame. Instead of being a military genius—an instrument of destruction and murder, as the profession of arms implies that a leader should be—General Mitchell, in my opinion, was the reverse. He sought to accomplish great results, great ends by far-reaching calculations of strategy, by means that would, if possible, avoid the sanguinary clash of arms, and the death-struggle on the battle-field.

The organ of destructiveness must be large in the successful soldier, and the general who lacks it, lacks one of the first qualifications in his profession. War is but the measurement of the power of brute force and strategy between two contending nations or armies, and the power of one or the other must be broken before there is a permanent and satisfactory peace. So the general who can inflict the greatest slaughter and destruction on his adversary in the shortest time is greatest in his profession—greatest in the art of peace, and, for ought I know, the greatest humanitarian, although I am aware my last assertion is open to enlightened controversy.

Measured by this rule, General Mitchell would not have taken rank among the most successful commanders, although he possessed many military qualifications in an eminent degree. Although he was a West Point graduate, in the same class with Lee and Joe Johnston, and knew the theory of war, yet it was a profession distasteful to him, and he had sought the more congenial field of letters and science, in which he distinguished himself. He was, at the time of his enlistment, a professor of mathematics, philosophy and astronomy in a Cincinnati college.

Had this unfortunate expedition, which he organized, been a success—and how narrowly it came to being a success the reader is already aware—General Mitchell would have been at once pronounced one of the best military strategists of the war, and his name and fame would have stood pre-eminent among military commanders. Even as it was, the rebels feared him, for, as they often said, there was never any telling what devilment "old star-gazing Mitchell" was up to. For the energy and enterprise he displayed in this independent command of a division, in which he accomplished large, though temporary, results, President Lincoln made him a Major General. He was a good judge of men; he was prompt and decisive, and foresaw events, almost with the power of intuition, and the details of his plans were made out almost with mathematical precision, and in this last was he very liable to be often at fault. Military operations must always be adjusted, or adjust themselves, to circumstances, weather, roads, and the movements of the enemy included.

General Mitchell had as much confidence in the success of our expedition, as a general could have. He was even enthusiastic, because he had planned it all out with all the careful details that he would in fore-telling the coming of a comet or an eclipse, and yet something told him—forewarned him—that that there was miscalculation somewhere—that we were doomed men—that he should never see us again, and, in the honesty of his nature, he told us so. He had implicit confidence in Andrews—in his fidelity, courage and sagacity. As showing General Mitchell's anxiety for the success of the expedition and the importance he attached to it, he promised Andrews fifty thousand dollars reward if he succeeded, although of this we knew nothing at the time, and Andrews would have received the money, for General Mitchell would never have made such a promise without assurance from some higher authority, probably the Secretary of War, or the Chief Agent of the Secret Service fund. The General believed that we would capture the train at Big Shanty as much as he believed in his existence, and he cautioned Andrews to avoid bloodshed if possible—not to kill the engineer and fireman if their lives could be spared. He, on his part, was prompt and on time in his advance movement on the railroad near Huntsville, but he had miscarried in one of the plainest and simplest matters—namely, giving sufficient time for our journey to Marietta, or rather, to Chattanooga. The heavy rains which suddenly came and the swollen rivers had not been included in his careful plan. It was a slight but fatal miscalculation.

I have been led into these comments, for which I ask the reader's pardon, in order to place more fully before all the exact relation which General Mitchell bore to this expedition. I have heard him condemned for permitting it, and have heard him charged with recklessness and selfish ambition for distinction, but I believe the reader, after having all the facts placed before him, will agree with me in my estimate of his honorable character. So far as my criticism of his soldierly genius goes, it is only my opinion—the humble opinion of a private soldier—and if I have erred in judgment, there are plenty of abler cotemporary soldier pens to correct me. I have felt this much due to the patriotic, loyal man who gave existence to the ill-fated adventure, in the carrying out of which I and my comrades suffered so much. Peace to his noble spirit.

We found good quarters at Port Royal and were royally treated by the eastern soldiers who were stationed there, and who understood and had the conveniences for making themselves about as comfortable as soldiers could well be. We soon got a chance to ship by small steamer to Hilton Head, twelve miles away, and soon after shipped thence to New York, on a large transport steamer, *The Star of the South*, which was in Government employ. On board was also the coffin containing the last remains of General Mitchell, which was being sent to his friends in Ohio. We had a pleasant voyage to New York, but did not stay long in the great, busy metropolis. Commander Crossman, and in fact, the officers at all the stations, had advised us to go immediately to Washington, and personally see the Secretary of War, and lay all the facts we were in possession of before him. So we secured transportations, at military headquarters in New York, to Washington.

We were detained in Baltimore, as we went through, until the Commissary General could find time to fix up our papers. The people were so hospitable, and officers, soldiers and everybody else treated us so well, that we remained for a couple of days. The newspaper men got hold of us, and soon it was noised everywhere that two of Mitchell's spies and bridge-burners had arrived direct from the heart of old Jeff's dominions, and Mark and I used to read the startling headlines with many a broad, good laugh to ourselves. We had free tickets to the theatres, museums and other public places, free rides and free lunches, and we began to wonder if we were not "bigger men than old Grant," or some other general.

But we had a great anxiety to get back to the regiment and learn how the fortunes of war had been with our old comrades and if any of the poor fellows who had broke jail with us had ever reached "God's country." All these things were a sealed book to us. We knew that battles had been fought, and that many a comrade had fallen. Any soldier, who has ever been a prisoner, will remember what an anxiety there is after months of absence, to learn the fate of those in the regiment at the front. It was so with us, and from the hour we came out within railroad communication of the army, I was restless and wanted to get back, and each day my anxiety increased.

When we arrived in Washington, Mark went to the Soldiers' Home to take up temporary quarters, and I started out to find the Commissary-General's office, to get transportation for us to our regiment, after which we proposed calling at the War Department. I thoughtlessly started out without a pass, not having been used to the strict patrol regulations in force in Washington at that time, and, as a natural consequence, had not gone far before I was confronted by a squad of nicely-dressed Provost guards, with bright new muskets, who "took me in," and not long after I had the mortification to see a prison door again closed on my liberty.

I did some audible soliloquizing after I was locked up, and it was not complimentary to Provost guards in general, nor to Washington in particular. What a reception, thought I, right here in the capital city of "God's country!" I almost wished I had remained at Baltimore. The most perplexing part of my dilemma was, that I did not know who to apply to, to get released. There was so much red tape about Washington military affairs, that I knew I was liable to spend several days and nights in the prison, if I went through the regulation course. It made me fairly boil over with vexation.

But a happy thought struck me. I had heard that President Lincoln was a very patient, kind man, and would give a hearing to a private soldier almost as readily as to an officer. I called for the officer in charge of the prison, who came in. He was a starchy, important kind of a man, who had, judging from appearances, never smelt rebel powder, unless it might, perhaps, have been on a woman's face, and was disposed to treat me as such officials were too much in the habit of treating private soldiers. He impatiently demanded to know "what I wanted."

I said, "Will you oblige me by sending me pen, ink and paper?"

"What do you want with paper?" said he.

"To write to the President," said I.

"And what in h—l have you to do with the President," said he.

I said, "It is no part of your duty or business to inquire into the matter."

He looked at me for a moment, and then condescendingly said, "All right, I will see that your wishes are complied with."

I hastily wrote a note, about as follows:

Mr. President:—I have just arrived in the city, fresh from a long imprisonment in Atlanta, Georgia, from which place of confinement I took ''French leave." The Provost guards have imprisoned me here, because I was found without a pass, in which, I suppose, they did but their duty. I know of no officer or friend in the city to whom I can apply for help. Can you do anything for me? If you can, you will greatly oblige your friend.

JOHN A. WILSON,
Of the Twenty-First Ohio Volunteer Infantry.

The messenger who took the note, which was addressed on the envelope, "A. Lincoln, President," had not been gone more than half an hour, until the prison door opened, and the starchy officer called my name. I came forward, and a pleasant, gentlemanly man, dressed in the clothes of a civilian, asked me if my name was Wilson. When I said it was, he took me by the hand and bid me walk out, at the same time handing the officer a written order for my release. The gentleman, who, probably, was the President's private secretary, told me that Mr. Lincoln requested that I should come and see him, and, that if I would accompany him, he would show me the way, and see that the

Provost guards did not molest me. When we arrived at the White House, my escort said, addressing Mr. Lincoln, "Mr. President, this is Mr. Wilson, one of the Mitchell railroad-raiders, who has just escaped from prison." The President came forward and took me by the hand, much in the manner a father would on receiving a long lost son. He said:

"Mr. Wilson, it affords me great pleasure to take you by the hand, and I thank God that your life has been spared."

He then conducted me forward to a table, where several gentlemen sat, to whom he introduced me, after which he showed me a seat. I was somewhat embarrassed, but I remember that Secretaries Seward and Chase were of the number. Mr. Seward, I recollect, seemed to be a serious, thoughtful looking old man, who said but very little, but listened attentively to the others. Mr. Lincoln sat down near me and manifested as much interest in me as if I had been an old and valued acquaintance. He congratulated me and my comrades for the spirit, determination and devotion we had shown, and the good luck which enabled us to escape. He seemed perfectly familiar with all the details of our expedition—the cause of its failure, and the good results that would have arisen from its success. "What a pity," continued the President, "that General Mitchell did not give you boys one more day to make your journey in. Had he done so, I have no doubt you would have succeeded. You all did your duty bravely and nobly and have suffered bitterly for it. The country owes each survivor a debt of gratitude, for which he should be suitably rewarded."

I told the President that my business in coming to Washington was to see him or the Secretary of War, and ask them to intercede for those of the expedition who were yet in captivity. He told me that Commander Crossman's dispatches had arrived at the War Department, and that steps had already been taken in behalf of the captives, by Secretary Stanton. He said that not another man of them should be harmed if the power of the Government could prevent it. "When you go back to your regiment," said the President, "tell your comrades, and tell them to send word to the friends of those men of the expedition now imprisoned, that Secretary Stanton, and through him the Government, has done, and is doing, and will continue to do, all that can be done to have them treated as regular prisoners of war, even if measures of retaliation are necessary."

In this declaration, as in all things he said and did, I believe the noble President was sincere, and I have no doubt, thought as sacredly of his word to me, an obscure private soldier, as he would if given to any influential general, or civil official. Of one thing I am certain. The men were never executed, but were treated like other prisoners, so far as I could learn. As he shook hands with me, when I took my leave, Mr. Lincoln said, "Each member of your expedition shall have a commission, and if the Governor of Ohio does not give you a commission, Mr. Wilson, I will give you a lieutenant's commission in the regular army."

A man was sent with me to the Commissary-General's office, where I secured passes and transportation for Mark and myself to go to our regiment, or to stop in Ohio until we received orders from the regiment, as we saw proper. We decided to go right through to the army of the Cumberland, as fast as we could, stopping only in Ohio long enough to shake hands with our friends and let them know that we were yet in the land of the living, and also to get a little money to bear our incidental expenses on our journey southward.

CHAPTER XVIII.

Returning to the Regiment—Back to the Army of the Cumberland—The Greeting of Old Comrades—Meeting with Captain Fry—History of Different Members of Our Party—Interesting Account from Wm. J. Knight—J. R. Porter's Account—Whereabouts of other Comrades of the Expedition—A FewWords Personal—Medal and Extra PayConcluding Words—A Hope that the Spirit of Rebellion is at an End.

WE reached our regiment a few days after the battle of Stone River. The men were camped near Murfreesboro, and only about twenty miles from Shelbyville, where we had left them nine months before. Our old comrades received us almost as two who had come to them from the dead.

They were not more rejoiced than we were, for after so long an absence and the many ups and downs and rough experiences we had met in the Confederacy, we felt, indeed, about as much joy and gratitude as two fellows could well live through in one day. Many beloved comrades, whose voices and faces were once familiar about the camp-fire and mess, were absent to come back no more. They slept their last long sleep, among the new-made graves, over in the cedars yonder. Their lives went out amid the din of battle, on the bloody field of Stone River. The remembrance of those absent ones, never to come again to roll-call with us, made me feel sad, but there is almost always some silver lining to the dark clouds in a soldier's life, and so it was with us.

One of the pleasantest surprises in store for me, was nothing less than the meeting with Captain Fry, "The noblest Roman of them all," whom I supposed was certainly dead. What a change had come over him since, bareheaded, starved, ragged and bony, I saw him seize Turner, the jailer, at the prison-door, on that never-to be-forgotten night, and hold him with the firm grip of a giant. Then, afterwards, as I ran for my life, away out, nearly a half mile from the prison, I caught a glimpse of Captain Fry, staggering and stumbling, as if about to fall, as I supposed, from the effects of a bullet-wound. Now, as I saw him, he was a robust, well-fed, soldierly, noble-looking man, but in heart, courage, manliness and nobility of character, the same man who had been our faithful comrade in prison. As a soldier, possessing great rugged qualities of mind and heart, he would have been a fit associate for Frederick the Great. He was with his regiment, the Third Tennessee, when I last saw him, and I know of few men living to-day (if he is living), for whom I entertain greater respect than Captain David Fry.

As the reader, who has followed my story thus far, will have an interest in knowing the fate of all our party of raiders who broke jail, I will as briefly and as correctly as possible, speak of each. Of our party of twenty-two, who had landed at Marietta, eight, as will be remembered, had been hung, leaving fourteen, who were in the Atlanta prison at the time of the break. Of these, eight made good their escape, and, after untold, hardships and suffering, reached the Federal lines.

Their names and present places of residence as far as I know, are as follows:

M. J. Hawkins, residence unknown.

D. A. Dorsey, Nebraska.

W. W. Brown, Wood County, Ohio.

William J. Knight, North Pacific Junction, Minnesota.

John Wollam, residence unknown.

John R. Porter, Carlisle, Arkansas.

Mark Wood, deceased.

These, with myself, include all who made good their escape. Brown, Knight and Mason kept together at the time of their flight from the prison, and from a very interesting account of his escape, sent me by Mr. Knight since I began the publication of these sketches, and who will be remembered as one of our engineers, I make an extract as follows:

WILLIAM J. KNIGHT'S ACCOUNT.

"We broke jail October 16, 1862, and scattered and scampered for the woods. W. W. Brown, E. H. Mason and myself, all of the Twenty-First Ohio Infantry, were together. The first night out, Mason took sick, and we did not get far, but kept well hidden. We were three days within nine miles of Atlanta. On the third night, Mason was so bad that we were compelled to go to a house with him, and began to despair of making good our escape; but he told us to leave him and save ourselves. Just as we had finished a hasty meal in the kitchen, three men came in at the front door to arrest us. They asked us if we were not some of the prisoners who broke jail in Atlanta. We told them we were. They said they had come to take us back, and that there was no use trying to escape, as all the roads and bridges were guarded.

"Brown was mad in an instant, and ripped out a very blunt reply. He said, 'I'll be d—d if you take us back, now see if you do!' At this Brown and I sprang out of the back door and ran round the end of the house and down a fence in the direction of some woods. They ran out of the front door with their shot-guns and bawled out, 'Halt! halt!' as we were leaving them on a 2:40 run. They straddled their horses and galloped out on a by-road from the house to the main road, while the man where we had stayed, unloosed his hounds, and they were soon on our trail in full cry. We had changed our course to baffle the horsemen, for there was a hill to go down and another to ascend before we got across the plantation and to the woods beyond. The men could not see us, but the cry of the dogs told our course, and before we had reached the woods the whole pack were closing on us. The field was full of loose stones, and we hastily chose the best place we could, and engaged in a savage combat with the dogs, in which we were victorious, crippling and driving away the whole pack in short order, after which we started again on full run.

"We could, by this time, see the horsemen coming round to head us off. We changed our course and threw them off again. The hounds followed at a long distance, and by their howling, indicated our course, but did not come near enough to molest us. We kept see-sawing and tacking to avoid the horsemen, who were doing their best to head us off, until, at last, we came to a little creek, in which we waded a couple of hours, and in this way caused the dogs to lose us. That day we reached Stone Mountain, eighteen miles east of Atlanta. After that we traveled nights, going due northward, with the north star for our guide. From our hiding places in the daytime we frequently saw scouting parties patroling the country, no doubt for the jail fugitives.

"We crossed the Chattahooche, October twenty-sixth, on rails tied together with bark. From the house where we left Mason, and ate breakfast in the kitchen, we were six days without food, except nuts and brush. On the seventh day we caught a goose and ate it raw, and on the same day found a few ears of corn left in the field by the huskers. This lasted until a day or so after, when we found a tree of apples which had not been gathered, probably because of their worthlessness. But they tasted good to us, and we filled up on them, and carried away all we could.

"Fortunately for us, the same day we discovered a drove of young hogs in the woods. I hid behind a tree with a club, and Brown tolled a confiding pig up near me, by biting off bits of apple and tossing them to it, backing up, meantime, until the young porker came within reach of my stick, when I murdered it. We split it up with a knife we had made from a piece of thin iron from a shovel handle, which iron we had sharpened by rubbing it on a stone. That night we found where some men had been clearing and burning, and we had a feast of cooked pork, without seasoning, but we enjoyed it without complaint, for, except the goose and corn, we had eaten only five meals in twenty-one days. The pig lasted us until we reached the Hiawasse River, near the corner of North Carolina.

"This was an intolerably rough country, and we traveled hard for four days, and only gained eight miles, during which time we saw no one, either to molest us or let us alone, and we were tramping along pretty bravely. We were crossing a little old clearing, which had a deserted appearance, when we came unexpectedly and suddenly out in front of a log house, where two men stood on the porch. They saw us and it was too late for us to dodge, so we tried to appear indifferent, and went up and asked if we could get dinner. We told them we were rebel soldiers, who had been on the sick list, and were trying to get back to our regiment. They said we could have dinner, and as we sat down to eat, the woman of the house, who seemed to be the mother of the two men, eyed us pretty closely. She was very talkative, and it was not long before she accused us of being Yanks. To make quite a long story short, we soon found each other out. They were loyal, true people, who fed and secreted us and sent us on to other friends, who in turn helped us to others, and so on, until we arrived at Somerset, Kentucky, about November twenty-fifth, from which place we reached Louisville, and from there by railroad to Nashville, near which place our old comrades and regiment lay, and where the boys received us with three times three and a tiger. Thus ended our adventures."

Mr. John R. Porter, formerly of Wood County, but now residing in Prairie County, Arkansas, publishes the following account of his adventures from the time the train left Marietta until he was imprisoned in Chattanooga:

JOHN R. PORTER'S ACCOUNT.

"Through some mistake or negligence of the hotel porter we were not called in time for the train, as it left quite early, although we arrived at the depot in time to see the train before it was out of sight. We gazed intently until the smoke of the iron-horse disappeared in the morning twilight. I cannot describe my feelings at that moment. I glanced at Hawkins, who appeared to be as much bewildered as myself. There we were in the heart of the Confederacy, knowing that if we were suspected of anything wrong death would be our portion. We could hardly make up our minds how to meet the emergency as we had to be very careful not to make any move that would create suspicion.

"Then we leisurely strolled about the town expecting every moment to hear of the capture of the train. Nor did we have to wait long, for the news soon reached the town that a train had been captured at Big Shanty, while the passengers and crew were at breakfast, and it was done so quickly and easily that they could not imagine who did the deed, or what it meant. Soon everything was wild with excitement, and the town was thronged with excited rebels, waiting to hear further developments regarding the wild train, as it was termed. Hawkins and I concluded to skip out, one at a time, though keeping sight of each other, and make our way to the country unmolested, if possible. In this we succeeded, and after reaching a piece of woods we came together, congratulated ourselves upon our success thus far, but what to do next we hardly knew. We felt certain, that the chances for our getting away in the present state of excitement, were not the best, and after much hesitation and doubt we determined to go to Big Shanty or Camp McDonald, as it was a rebel camp of instruction, and join the rebel army, and thus be enabled to make our escape, when sent to the front, by deserting a picket-post or taking the first opportunity that might offer for escape in any way. We proceeded on our way, intending to reach Camp McDonald about sundown, thinking perhaps that by this time the excitement would be somewhat subsided.

"We came in sight of the town late in the day and marched into camp and reported at headquarters. Here we found several rebel officers, one of whom, who bore the marks of a Colonel, turned his attention to us. After a short interview, which seemed plausible to him, he ordered us to report to the commanding officer of the Ninth Georgia Battalion for enlistment. One of the companies, not being full, was called into line and took a vote whether or not we should be received into the company. The vote was unanimous in our favor, and we, after giving fictitious names, were assigned to a certain mess for our suppers. After supper we made the acquaintance of some of our new mess-mates, relating dismal stories of our treatment by the 'Yankee' hirelings in Kentucky, which made a good impression on our comrades as to our loyalty to the Confederacy.

"Everything went all right with us until in some manner it leaked out among the rebels that the Yankee raiders, by mistake or accident, had left two of their party at Marietta. How this information got out I never learned, but it could not be otherwise than that *some one of our party had indiscreetly told more than he ought to when captured; who the man was we never learned.* The excitement ran very high, and we discovered, when it was too late, that we had run into the very jaws of danger, for immediately we fell under suspicion and were sent to headquarters and there ordered to give a truthful account of ourselves, under the penalty of death if we lied. We were taken into a room, one at a time, and interviewed by a number of rebel officers—Hawkins first and myself afterwards. When Hawkins came out I saw at a glance that something was wrong; but my turn had come and I took my seat in the room, confronted by six Confederate officers, when I put on the boldest front I could.

"One of the officers, a Colonel, took me in hand and began by first inquiring my name, which I did not give in full, as I had given my name John Reed when I enlisted. He proceeded in his order of examination as best suited him, and I answered as best suited myself, just the reverse of what they desired. Finally, others of the party commenced asking questions and I found that I was in a pretty tight place. On various occasions during nearly four years of army life I experienced some pretty close calls, and run the gauntlet frequently, but this was a little the closest corner I ever got into. They were very menacing and abusive, expecting, I suppose, to scare me into a confession.

"The Colonel finally said, 'Mr. Reed, you stand there thrice damned. You may make your peace with your God, but you never can with Jeff. Davis, and we ought to hang you without any further ceremony.'

"I was permitted to return to the room with Hawkins, where we were closely guarded, and were not allowed to converse with each other. The word soon spread through the camp that we were 'Yankees,' and belonged to the railroad party. In a short time the building was surrounded with an excited mob that demanded our immediate execution—some threatening to shoot us and some to hang us before we should leave there. As they still gathered around, the excitment increased, until they placed a heavy guard around the building, and the crowd soon began to disperse, intent upon a fresh attack at night.

"As soon as the first train came along going South, we were put aboard under guard and sent to Marietta, where we were hand-cuffed and chained together by the end of a trace-chain being placed around the neck of each and locked with padlocks. Then, to make assurance doubly sure, we were placed in an inner cell of the jail for safe keeping during the night. The news soon spread through the town of our arrival, and, in a short time an infuriated mob gathered around the jail and demanded our release, that they might wreak out their vengeance upon us, otherwise they would burn the jail. As the night wore on the crowd increased until they finally placed another heavy guard around the jail; that somewhat allayed our fears for the remainder of the night. That night, with its blackness and darkness, will long be remembered by me as I hardly closed my eyes during the night, and it seemed as though morning never would come. When it did come, however, the jail was again surrounded by curiosity seekers and a mob-spirited crowd, to see the wild 'Yankees,' as they called us.

"During the morning we were hurried to the depot under a strong guard to protect us from the mob, and were put aboard for Chattanooga, where we were put into 'old Swim's hotel,' or more properly 'the hole,' where we found eight of our old comrades who had preceded us into this horrible den."

John R. Porter, also of the Twenty-First Regiment, and John Wollam, of the Thirty-Third, who passed so near to where Wood and I lay under the bushes on the night of the escape, struck westward, and after one month and two days of almost incredible hardship, reached the Federal lines at Corinth, Mississippi.

Hawkins and Dorsey, of the Thirty-Third Regiment, after a very similar experience of hunger and privation, reached some Union friends in the Cumberland mountains, who aided them to reach the Federal forces in Kentucky.

Mason, of the Twenty-First, now a resident of this State, who escaped with Brown and Knight, and was taken sick, was recaptured, as also was William Bensinger, of the same regiment, and who is also a resident of Ohio.

Of the other four of the six who did not succeed in making good their escape, I have but little present information. Robert Buffum, poor fellow, once an enthusiastic anti-slavery soldier and compatriot with old John Brown, in Kansas, died, I regret to learn, by his own hand, some three years since.

Jacob Parrott, the heroic young soldier who was so brutally whipped, is a resident of Kenton, Ohio, and is physically, like most of the others of the party, a mere wreck, with broken health.

I have no tidings of William Reddick, of the Thirty-Third Regiment.

William Pittenger, of the Second Ohio Regiment, I learn, is leading a useful life in the ministry at Vineland, New Jersey. These six prisoners were changed to a safer prison, and through the efforts, no doubt, of the War Department and Secretary Stanton, were afterwards sent to Richmond, from which latter place they were sent out to Fortress Monroe, in the latter part of March, 1863, almost a year from the time they were captured, when they were regularly exchanged with other prisoners.

Several prisoners from East Tennessee made their escape at the same time, whom I have never heard of since. One poor fellow, named Barlow, was shot through the knee in the fight with the guards at the jail, or had his leg broken in some manner. The rebel guards bayoneted him back into prison, and let him die by inches, refusing him any medical attendance. His sufferings must have been terrible. Mr. Pittenger, in his published account, says that the commandant, Colonel Lee, in giving orders to those troops whom he sent in pursuit of the escaped prisoners, said to them, "Don't take one of the villains alive! Shoot them down, and let them lie in the woods for the hogs to eat!" Mr. Pittenger was told shortly after, that several of the escaped men had been shot and left in the woods. But, fortunately, this was not true. Yet it seems almost marvelous that some were not killed outright at the jail, and that more than half of our number escaped, when the distance to the Federal lines is considered.

Now a few words personal, for which I beg the reader's pardon, and I am done. After joining my regiment I was detailed for detached duty, and remained at Fort Rosecrans, Murfreesboro, during the remainder of my term of enlistment, at the expiration of which I was discharged, at Atlanta, Georgia, in 1864. Each member of our party, by act of Congress, received a medal. We also were given $100 extra pay, which was presented by General Rosecrans, at his headquarters, in Murfreesboro. I do not know whether the money was sent us by act of Congress, or was a private donation from Secretaries Chase and Stanton. I have heard the matter stated both ways.

I have been asked, since I began publishing this story, if I ever received a commission or a pension. I have never received either. I suppose there is a commission, of old date, for me in the Adjutant General's office of Ohio. I have never called for it. When I came out of the army, I was unfit for service, and did not consider myself fit for a soldier, either as officer or private. Some of our party received their commissions, and others never had a chance to apply for them, or, if they did, never cared enough about them to reap the benefit.

Before concluding this final, chapter, I wish to avail myself of the opportunity to thank the editor and employees of the *Wood County Sentinel* for their patience, kindness and forbearance in the publication of my sketches, and to the correspondents and many readers of the *Sentinel* for their appreciative, indulgent, kind, encouraging notices and words.

My story has been rather a long one—longer than I intended. It has been mostly a story of sorrow and suffering—"a cloud without a silver lining," but I could not tell it truthfully and have it otherwise; gladly would I have had it different. This story of hardship tells but a millionth part of what the war cost this people, and were I to be summoned to my last earthly account to-day, it would be a soothing consciousness to know—to feel, that the deadly strife which ceased at Appomattox Court House will never appear anew, under any other form, backed and sustained by the same rankling, anti-loyal spirit, whose hatred knew no limits in brutal deeds of blood, less than a score of years ago. I fear that the same blood-thirsty passion still slumbers. The bitterness and anguish of defeat and disappointment still rankle and burn in Ambition's blighting, destroying crucible. Give these men the power, and the most sanguine friends of an undivided government will have cause to tremble.

I am not unforgiving; I am not revengeful. I was so once, and I have sought those who wronged me, and murdered my comrades in cold blood, with violent intent. I felt that they ought to be punished. I am willing to forgive much of the past; but the Christian spirit of forgiveness is one thing, and trusting one's self in the hands of a bitter, treacherous, deadly enemy is quite another. Go to the heart of the late Confederacy, and see and feel the crushing, murderous, grinding despotism, born of ignorance and hatred of free institutions, as I have, and, dear friend and patient reader, you will agree with me that it is not safe to be hasty in putting those men in power in high places. It is this tendency in our Government, and in the two great political parties of the day, that makes me say that I would like to feel certain that rebellious strife will never be renewed. I pray that it may not be.

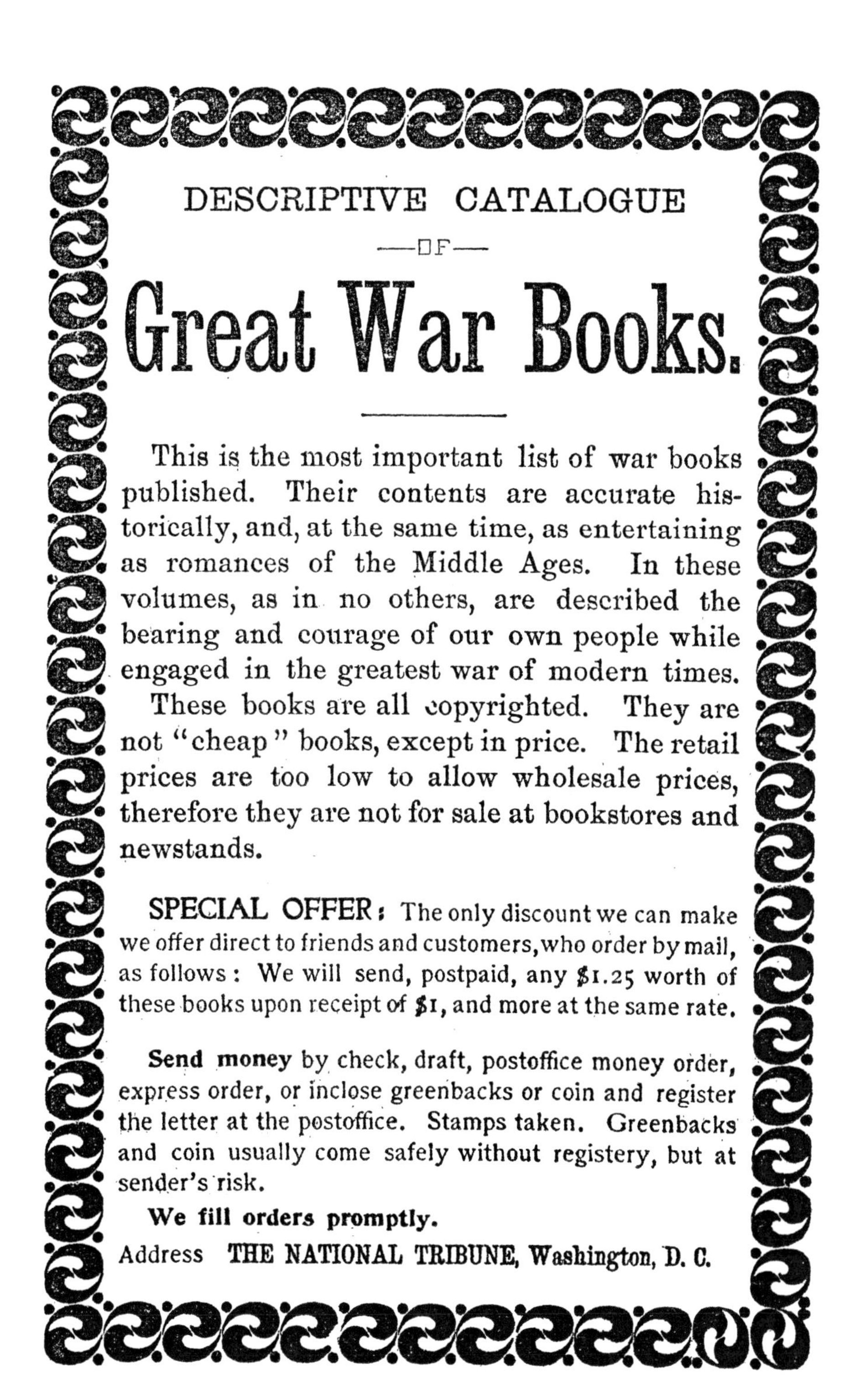
DESCRIPTIVE CATALOGUE
—OF—
Great War Books.
This is the most important list of war books published. Their contents are accurate historically, and, at the same time, as entertaining as romances of the Middle Ages. In these volumes, as in no others, are described the bearing and courage of our own people while engaged in the greatest war of modern times.
These books are all copyrighted. They are not "cheap" books, except in price. The retail prices are too low to allow wholesale prices, therefore they are not for sale at bookstores and newstands.
SPECIAL OFFER: The only discount we can make we offer direct to friends and customers, who order by mail, as follows: We will send, postpaid, any $1.25 worth of these books upon receipt of $1, and more at the same rate.
Send money by check, draft, postoffice money order, express order, or inclose greenbacks or coin and register the letter at the postoffice. Stamps taken. Greenbacks and coin usually come safely without registery, but at sender's risk.
We fill orders promptly.
Address THE NATIONAL TRIBUNE, Washington, D. C.

SI KLEGG.

His Transformation from a Raw Recruit to a Veteran.

Most Entertaining Book Ever Printed. Large Type; 320 Pages; Leatherette Cover.

Profusely Illustrated by the Inimitable Coffin, whose Pictures Vividly Portray Every Changing Scene of the Text.

ORDER—ARMS!"

THE TRANSFORMATION OF MORE THAN 2,000,000 young, brave, enthusiastic, but wholly undisciplined, American boys into hardy, seasoned veterans, the equals of which the world never saw, is always a story of the most fascinating interest.

It was a process full of the most terrible earnestness to every boy who underwent it, yet its most trying incidents frequently abounded in the most ludicrous features, at which no one laughed more heartily than the boy himself after he graduated in the grand school of actual war.

No account of these experiences has ever approached the widespread popular favor extended to "Si Klegg and Shorty." The sketches were written by one who as a boy had actually gone through the fullest measure of the experience, either for himself or his immediate comrades. He described them so well and vividly that every veteran in the country at once recognized them as his own—a faithful portrayal of the ordeal through which he had himself gone. They told exactly what he underwent in becoming a real soldier better than he could do it himself. They revived a thousand fading memories of the camp, the drill-ground, the march and the battlefield. They took him through every changing experience, from the feelings with which he signed his name to the enlistment roll and started from his dear old home, to his tribulations in learning the drill and regulations, in accustoming himself to the Government rations and slumbering on the soft side of a rail, to the fatigues of the march and the awful strain of battle.

These sketches have been laughed at and cried over in 10,000 homes of veterans, in Post rooms, at campfires, and wherever the survivors of the war have gathered together by twos or threes or by hundreds.

Price, postpaid to any address, 25 cents.

Address THE NATIONAL TRIBUNE, Washington, D. C.

FURTHER MISHAPS

TO

SI AND SHORTY.

BY JOHN McELROY.

Illustrated with Hundreds of Illustrations by Klemroth.

448 Pages; Leatherette Cover.

SI'S "PAP" ON THE WAY TO THE FRONT.

CORPORAL SI KLEGG AND HIS COMrade Shorty have become historic characters. They are the embodiment of the patriotic Union soldier who went into the army in 1861 and fought through the war to the finish. Their experiences form those of the raw recruit, and in the course of time the seasoned veteran. They pass through the vicissitudes of the unwelcome discipline incident to the transformation of a country boy into a soldier.

They encounter the dangers of the battlefield and the weariness of the tiresome march. Under all these circumstances these boys do their part manfully, having their ups and downs, their hard times and their good times, with a succession of comical blunders, brilliant achievements and stirring adventures which make up the panorama of a soldier's daily life.

Several new characters are introduced in this volume. Among them may be mentioned the Jew Spy and Deacon Klegg, Si's "pap," who visits the army to see the boys, and falls into many trying places, from all which, however, the old man's hard sense and good fortune combined extricate him, and he goes back full of experiences to relate to "mother and the girls."

This book will be keenly appreciated by those who received a previous volume treating of the early military career of our heroes, under the title of "Si Klegg." This record is simply the continuation of the same story, although it treats of a different period of the war.

Alexander Dumas or Charles Lever never wrote a more interesting book descriptive of a soldier's life than is here presented by the author of "The Further Mishaps to Si and Shorty."

Price, postpaid to any address, 25 cents.

Address THE NATIONAL TRIBUNE, Washington, D. C.

THE BOY SPY IN DIXIE.

Service Under the Shadow of the Scaffold.

By J. O. KERBEY.

Fully Illustrated by the Surpassing Skill of Coffin. Large Type; 384 Pages; Leatherette Cover.

"I SURRENDER!"

THE MYSTERY WHICH ENSHROUDS the life of a spy is one of the never-fading charms of the stories of war. The experiences of the men who take their lives in their hands when they enter the contest of subterfuge, risking death in the battle of wit and deceit, fall upon ears that never tire. Stories of such adventures have the same fascination which attend the exploits of freebooters, the daring of navigators in unknown seas and the doings of hunters in untrodden wilds.

Such a narrative is the one told by the Boy Spy in Dixie. It is a relation of stirring episodes among enemies, in the face of the gibbet. The author, while a mere youth, was sent by the great War Secretary into the heart of the Confederacy.

Here in the midst of constant peril he watched the doings of Jeff Davis and his Cabinet and the Confederate Congress, and by means of a correspondence in cypher sent forward day by day to the Government at Washington the reports of his observations. His experiences were varied and trying. At times he was in the confidence of those high in authority in the Confederacy, and again an object of suspicion. Finally, by stress of circumstances, he was compelled to enlist and become a Confederate artilleryman; and, being ordered with the command to Cumberland Gap, deserted from the rebel army and escaped into Kentucky, finding his way once more to the protection of the Union flag. No sooner had he reported at Washington, however, than he was again sent on a perilous expedition within the Confederate lines at Fredericksburg, and once more found himself in Richmond. Every day added to his jeopardy. He was not only a Union spy, but a rebel deserter.

In the midst of all his perils, however, our author found time for passages of gallantry among the Southern belles, and incidentally we are given vivid glimpses of social life at Richmond and Fredericksburg that might well grace the pages of a novel dealing in the arts of love rather than the cruelties of war.

Having escaped all these desperate chances and saved his neck, the "Boy Spy" now, a generation after the scenes have past, gives to us a thrilling story rich with detail, wherein he tells what he saw and how he escaped the fate which he dared day after day.

Price, postpaid to any address, 25 cents.

Address THE NATIONAL TRIBUNE, Washington, D. C.

"THE CANNONEER."

BY AUGUSTUS BUELL.

Story of a Private Soldier.

Fully and Graphically Illustrated; 384 Pages; Leatherette Cover.

THE CANNONEER IS A WONDERFUL book, such as very rarely appears in literature. It is one that appeals directly to the popular heart—to all who love and admire courage, loyalty, and devoted service. The author was a volunteer, but early in his service was transferred to one of the finest batteries in the Regular Army, and which did some of the very hardest fighting in the War of the Rebellion. From Antietam to Appomattox it was constantly engaged, and nearly always in the very forefront of battle. Its terrible fighting at Antietam, Gettysburg, and Bethesda Church was unprecedented in the history of light artillery.

The attention is caught at the very first and held to the end. The men—Generals, battery officers and privates—whom he describes are pictured so admirably that they become personal acquaintances and friends, and the reader gets breathlessly interested in them. The scenes of camp and march are wonderfully true to life, and call up a flood of memories in the breast of every old soldier.

The features of the book are:

1. The real life and experiences of a private soldier in a fighting battery.

2. Wonderfully fresh and vivid descriptions of the battles of Antietam, Gettysburg, the Wilderness, Spottsylvania; the terrible fighting from there to the James River; the short-range duel with a rebel battery, which was destroyed; the assaults on the rebel lines at Petersburg; the months of fighting and digging in front of that stronghold; the battles of Opequan and Cedar Creek, in the Shenandoah Valley; the decisive little battle at Five Forks, which forced Lee out of his works; the relentless pursuit of the rebel army, and the surrender at Appomattox. All this is clearly told.

3. Carefully-drawn diagrams of the various battlefields, corrected from the War Department's surveys.

4. A vast number of new facts and figures regarding those battles, the numbers of the opposing forces, the organizations on both sides, and the losses.

Price, postpaid to any address, 25 cents.

Address **THE NATIONAL TRIBUNE, Washington, D. C.**

CAPTURING A LOCOMOTIVE.

A True History of the Most Thrilling and Romantic Secret Service of the Late War.

By REV. WILLIAM PITTENGER,

One of the Actors in the Strange Scenes Described, and now a Minister of the Methodist Episcopal Church.

Fully Illustrated; 350 Pages; Leatherette Cover.

THE STORY OF THE BOOK.

THIS IS, UNDOUBTEDLY, THE MOST thrilling book of the great civil war. The enterprise described possesses all the unity of a drama from the first plunge of the actors into the enemy's country, through all their adventures and changing fortunes, until the few survivors stood once more under the old flag. No single war story vividly presents so many of the hidden, underground elements of the struggle against rebellion as this. From beginning to end the reader's attention never wearies, and he rises from the perusal feeling almost as if he had again lived through those terrible days. The adventurers traversed the Confederacy in all directions; some perished as spies, all suffered terribly, and the wonder is that any escaped alive.

Three events narrated in the story of this expedition are unparalleled either in ancient or modern warfare. No writer of romance would dare to invent the capture of a crowded railroad train in the midst of an enemy's camp by a band of twenty unarmed soldiers who had journeyed hundreds of miles from their own lines. The subsequent escape of part of the same band by seizing an armed guard almost in sight of a regiment of foes, and stealthily crossing the whole breadth of the Confederacy in different directions, is equally marvelous; while the sad tragedy that occurred at Atlanta is freshly and vividly remembered by the inhabitants of that beautiful city after a lapse of more than thirty years. The claim of this whole "Railroad Adventure" to be regarded as the most remarkable episode of the civil war has never been disputed.

TABLE OF CONTENTS.

Price, postpaid to any address, 25 cents.

Address THE NATIONAL TRIBUNE, Washington, D. C.

THE
American Conflict

Practically a Complete History of Our Country as well as of the Great Rebellion.

BY HORACE GREELEY

Large 8vo.; Two Volumes; 1,430 Pages; 144 Steel Portraits and 80 Views, Maps and Plans of Battles.

ISING FROM THE HUMBLER WALKS OF LIFE, Horace Greeley for more than 50 years, by the force of his intellect, led popular thought in this country. While still in the prime of his powers he was enabled to look back over the most stormy period in our career as a people, and as the result of his observation and experience has left this priceless contribution to the annals of the Nation. This history is without a peer in our literature.

Mr. Greeley's history is not only the most faithful and fascinating chronicle of the War of the Rebellion extant, but it embraces likewise a complete history of the country, tracing its growth from the beginning, through all its political vicissitudes, up to the firing upon Fort Sumter, which heralded the opening of the most desperate struggle of modern times.

To the writing of this history Mr. Greeley brought the ripe scholarship of mature years as a result of the study of popular questions from the standpoint of an editor, speaker, and member of Congress. He was the intellectual giant of his generation.

The leatherette binding we use is of a superior quality, and will outwear ordinary cloth, and will permanently retain its beauty and finish.

The **original text is complete and unabridged,** exactly as in the high-priced editions, word for word.

The **original illustrations,** maps and plans of battlefields are reproduced exactly. There are 144 portraits on steel, and 80 other illustrations, including maps and plans of battlefields.

As a **GIFT** these Greeley volumes are most acceptable.

This is one of the very few historical works that is as fascinating as a novel. The young who read it will cultivate a taste for good books.

Without self-glorification we confess to a sense of pride in our accomplishment in being thus able to offer this great work upon terms which bring it within the reach of all who have heretofore failed to secure it on account of its exorbitant price, which ranged from $9 to $13, according to the binding.

No American who desires to talk intelligently of the history of his country, either as a public speaker or in private conversation, should fail to read and study these volumes.

Price for the two volumes, postpaid, $1. The sale of these volumes strictly limited to subscribers of THE NATIONAL TRIBUNE.

Tobys Army Depot.
Ulysses. Cannon.
(317) 363-8429.

Breinigsville, PA USA
26 April 2010
236802BV00001B/8/P

9 781582 187891